Costa del Sol

by Mona King

Mona King is a freelance travel writer. She has long-standing ties with Spain, once worked for the Spanish Tourist Office in London, and has travelled extensively throughout Spain, western Europe and Mexico. Author of AA Publishing's *Best Drives Spain* and *TwinPack Costa del Sol*, she has also written the AA *Tourguide Mexico* and AA-Thomas Cook *Travellers' Mexico*.

Above: *a bar in Marbella*

AA Publishing

An Andalusian

Written by Mona King

First published 1998. Reprinted Apr and Nov 1998; Mar 1999.
Second edition 2000. Reprinted Apr and Aug 2000; May 2001
Reprinted Apr 2002. Information verified and updated.
Reprinted Aug 2002
This edition 2005. Information verified and updated.
Reprinted May and Oct 2005
Reprinted Jan 2006
Reprinted Apr and Aug 2006

Published by AA Publishing, a trading name of Automobile Association Developments Limited, whose registered office is Fanum House, Basing View, Basingstoke, Hampshire, RG21 4EA. Registered number 1878835.

A03178

Colour separation: Keenes, Andover
Printed and bound in Italy by Printer Trento S.r.l.

Find out more about AA Publishing and the wide range of travel publications and services the AA provides by visiting our website at www.theAA.com/travel

Contents

About this Book

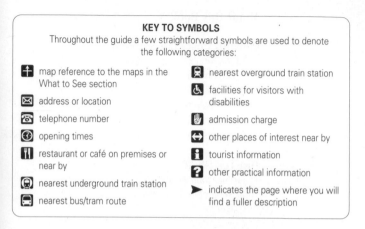

KEY TO SYMBOLS

Throughout the guide a few straightforward symbols are used to denote the following categories:

✚ map reference to the maps in the What to See section

✉ address or location

☎ telephone number

🕙 opening times

🍴 restaurant or café on premises or near by

Ⓜ nearest underground train station

🚌 nearest bus/tram route

🚆 nearest overground train station

♿ facilities for visitors with disabilities

✋ admission charge

↔ other places of interest near by

ℹ tourist information

❓ other practical information

➤ indicates the page where you will find a fuller description

---

This book is divided into five sections to cover the most important aspects of your visit to Costa del Sol.

Viewing Costa del Sol pages 5–14
An introduction to Costa del Sol by the author
    Costa del Sol's Features
    Essence of Costa del Sol
    The Shaping of Costa del Sol
    Peace and Quiet
    Costa del Sol's Famous

Top Ten pages 15–26
The author's choice of the Top Ten attractions in Costa del Sol, with practical information.

What to See pages 27–90
Two sections: Málaga and Costa del Sol & Beyond, each with brief introductions and an alphabetical listing of the main attractions
    Practical information
    Snippets of 'Did You Know…' information
    4 suggested walks
    4 suggested tours
    2 features

Where To… pages 91–116
Detailed listings of the best places to eat, stay, shop, take the children and be entertained.

Practical Matters pages 117–24
A highly visual section containing essential travel information.

Maps
All map references are to the individual maps found in the What to See section of this guide.
For example, the town of Casares has the reference ✚ 46A1 – indicating the page on which the map is located and the grid square in which the town is to be found. A list of the maps that have been used in this travel guide can be found in the index.

Prices
Where appropriate, an indication of the cost of an establishment is given by € signs:
€€€ denotes higher prices, €€ denotes average prices, while € denotes lower charges.

Star Ratings
Most of the places described in this book have been given a separate rating:
✪✪✪   Do not miss
✪✪   Highly recommended
✪   Worth seeing

Viewing Costa del Sol

Above: *locals on a balcony*
Right: *a bull advertises sherry*

Mona King's Costa del Sol

The Early Days

The first signs of tourism along this coast can be traced back to the early 19th century when the English discovered Málaga as a winter resort. However, it was at Torremolinos that the first hotels were built. The founding of the Marbella Club by Prince Alfonso von Hohenlohe of Liechtenstein played a key role in opening up the area to the jet set, putting it clearly on the social map. With its appeal to both the package tour market and the more discerning individual, the Costa del Sol has never looked back.

For many, mention of the Costa del Sol conjures up visions of suntanned bodies on the beach, luxurious hotels set in tropical gardens, golfing and glitzy marinas lined with millionaires' yachts, lively restaurants and swinging clubs – in other words, the high life, where you might rub shoulders with celebrities. Indeed, the Costa del Sol can offer all of this though, since its popularity took off in the 1960s and it became the 'in place' for the jet set, it has had its ups and downs. However, in recent years it has regained its position as a top year-round destination.

The ambience is cosmopolitan, and expatriates from all walks of life have settled here with a particularly high concentration around Torremolinos, Marbella and Fuengirola. The estimated figure for foreigners who live here, whether permanently or part-time, is over 400,000, mostly British, German, Dutch and Scandinavian.

Although the scene has changed with the times, the 'beautiful people' still come here. The tendency is now to seek more seclusion, however, with much of the entertaining and partying taking place in private. But the Costa del Sol still exudes an aura of glamour, which serves as a continuing magnet to visitors. Its mild, sunny winter climate, unrivalled in Europe, is an additional attraction.

From the late 1990s onwards there has been an effort to encourage visitors to look beyond the beach-only holiday, and to sample the more rural pleasures of the hinterland. The Costa del Sol is an excellent gateway to the beautiful interior of Andalucía with its enchanting white towns and villages dotted about the countryside, peaceful landscapes and its real jewels, the historic cities of Sevilla, Córdoba and Granada.

The popular holiday resort of Fuengirola has a special appeal for families

Costa del Sol's Features

Geography
• Although the Costa del Sol lies officially within the province of Málaga, but this book covers a more extended area, including the provinces of Granada and Cádiz, and the hinterland.
• The Costa del Sol covers nearly 300km of the Mediterranean coast.

Climate
• Average temperatures: spring 20°C, summer 28°C, autumn 18°C, winter 13°C.
• Average sea temperatures: 15°C in January, 24°C in August.
• A minimum 8 hours' sunshine is expected daily for 320 days a year.
• Most rainfall is likely to occur between December and March.

Agriculture
• The famous sweet Málaga wines are produced in Los Montes de Málaga Antequera, north of the city, and in La Axarquiá, to the east.
• Olive groves are a feature of the Andalucian landscape. Olive oil, which is refined in Málaga, rates among Spain's leading exports.
• Oranges and bananas, and acres of vegetables such as peppers, tomatoes and potatoes are cultivated along with wheat, sugarcane, tobacco and cotton.
• Cumin, coriander, cinnamon, marjoram, thyme and rosemary are among the herbs which flourish here.
• The uplands of the Guadalquivir are famous for black fighting bulls and thoroughbred horses.

Sport and Leisure
• Long sandy beaches stretch along the western Costa del Sol; east of Málaga you will come across smaller beaches and rocky coves.
• The Costa del Sol has over 50 golf courses.
• There are some 20 tennis clubs and most top-grade hotels have tennis courts.
• This stretch of coast boasts over 11 marinas.
• Many resorts offer sailing, waterskiing, windsurfing (top spot Punta de Tarifa) and scuba diving.
• Para cailing, hang gliding, delta-winging, and kitesurfing in some resorts, are also available.
• Skiing in the Sierra Nevada, Europe's most southerly ski resort, is an increasingly popular winter sport.
• Stables offer horse rides along and behind the coast.

Far from the crowded resorts, life in the rural areas continues in the old traditional ways

Roads
Take great care when driving on the N340.This continues to be a dangerous road, with traffic moving at great speed. Travelling time can be cut considerably by taking the toll-paying Autopista del Sol, which bypasses the major resorts.

Spices
When the Moors first arrived on the Iberian peninsula, they found the land poorly cultivated, lacking in fruit and other produce. Under the Omeya, the ruling class, dams, irrigation canals and water mills were built. Pepper, cinnamon, coriander and cumin were among the spices which were introduced, soon to spread to the medieval courts of Europe. Spices were highly valued for their preservative and medicinal properties.

Essence of Costa del Sol

The Costa del Sol is essentially about year-round fun and sun. With its long beaches, restaurants, bars, and choice of entertainment, it caters for all markets, from luxury to package tours. You can go for action, play golf or tennis, pursue your favourite water sports, or opt for the sweet life – poolside sunbathing and leisurely lunches by the sea or on a balcony, delightful on a warm, sunny day.

Above: *goats corralled on a hillside near Torrox*

Right: *seafront fishing boats of Torre del Mar*

Below: *Sevilla and Málaga are popular with flamenco fans*

THE 10 ESSENTIALS

If you only have a short time to visit Costa del Sol, or would like to get a really complete picture of the region, here are the essentials:

- **Do the daytime scene** in Puerto Banús. Linger over a drink at the Sinatra Bar or the Saladuba Pub and admire the yachts. Then move on for a long lunch at one of the stylish open-air restaurants on the quayside.
- **Enjoy fresh seafood** at any one of the *chiringuitos* (beach restaurants) in La Carihuela, Torremolinos.
- **Wander around** the picturesque old town of Marbella and round off with a drink in the Plaza de los Naranjos.
- **Visit Málaga** and do an evening round of the wealth of *tapas* bars centred in the old town.
- **Walk up to the Alcazaba and Gibralfaro** for the panoramic views over Málaga and the bay.
- **See a flamenco show** in Málaga or inland in Sevilla.
- **Have an evening drink** on Marbella's promenade and watch the sunset, taking in a wide view of the Rock of Gibraltar and coastline of Africa.
- **Do the rounds of Banús by night.** The action starts around midnight and

continues until dawn with dozens of discos, bars and clubs. Take your pick!
- **Drive up into the hills** to Mijas and enjoy the magnificent views.
- **Visit Ronda** to admire its stunning setting and famous old bridge, subject of countless paintings and photographs.
- **Highlights** include visits to the Alhambra in Granada, the Great Mosque at Córdoba and Sevilla, capital of Andalucía.

Top right: *Plaza de la Constitución, Fuengirola*

Right: *the dazzling image of Puerto Banús*

Left: *rooftops of old Antequera*

The Shaping of Costa del Sol

c25,000 BC
Paintings discovered in Nerja and Pileta caves show evidence of cave dwellers during this period.

4000 BC
Neolithic tribes from North Africa settle in southern Spain.

500 BC
The region is colonised by the Carthaginians.

210 BC
Following Roman domination, Andalucía is named Baetica. Málaga and Córdoba develop into important Roman towns.

AD 400
Decline of Roman Empire. The region is invaded by Vandals from northern Europe and named Vandalusia.

711
Moorish troops under the command of Tariq land in the south of Spain and begin the conquest of the peninsula. Moslem rule follows.

756
Al Andalus is converted into an emirate.

The flight of King Alfonso XIII in 1931 gave rise to the establishment of Spain's Second Republic

929
The independence of the Caliphate of Córdoba is proclaimed.

1031
The Caliphate is broken up into *tarifas* (small kingdoms).

1212
Christian victory at Las Navas de Tolosa (Jaén) marks a significant step in the reconquest of Andalucía.

1487
Armies of the Catholic Monarchs, Ferdinand and Isabella, conquer Málaga.

1492
Surrender of Granada to the Catholics ends Moorish rule in Spain. Banishment of Muslims and Jews.

1568
King Philip II takes measures against the Moriscos (Moors converted to Christianity) living in Málaga, who rebel and take refuge in the region of Las Alpujarras.

1610
Final expulsion of the Moriscos.

1704
British capture Gibraltar.

1808
The citizens of Málaga form a council to resist the French invaders, but the French advance and sack the city.

1812
The French are driven from Spain.

1873
Anarchy in Málaga. Attempts to set up an independent canton fail and the city is subdued by the government.

1931
King Alfonso XIII goes into exile. Unrest in Málaga.

1936
Uprising leads to the outbreak of civil war. The Nationalists take control of Sevilla, Córdoba, Granada. Málaga remains in the hands of the government.

1937
Málaga is taken by Nationalist forces.

1939
End of civil war with victory for General Franco; a period of hardship and poverty for the region over the next decade.

1950s
The start of investment in the Costa del Sol and the beginnings of mass tourism.

1975
Death of General Franco. King Juan Carlos I heads the return to constitutional monarchy and democracy

1982
Andalucía becomes one of Spain's 17 autonomous regions.

Tiles in Sevilla depicting the Christian Reconquest of Málaga

1985
The border with Gibraltar is reopened.

1992
Expo '92 held in Sevilla.

1997
Following a slump in tourism, a new era opens for the Costa del Sol with an ambitious investment programme.

2003
Opening of the new Picasso Museum in Málaga.

11

Peace & Quiet

For those who feel like taking a break from the hustle and bustle of the Costa del Sol, there are many possibilities. The hinterland offers a variety of landscapes, from olive groves in rolling hills, to dramatic mountain ranges with snowcapped peaks. In a very short time you can leave behind the heat of the coast and lose yourself in the tranquil surroundings of inland Andalucía.

Nature Parks and Reserves

The Coto de Doñana National Park is an important resting area for a great variety of migratory birds

Within reach of the coast are a number of protected areas and nature parks. With landscapes of wild natural beauty and a wealth of flora and fauna they make an ideal destination for the nature lover seeking peace and quiet.

Among these are the Parque Natural Montes de Málaga, north of Málaga; and south of Antequera, the Parque Natural Torcal de Antequera, which features weird and wonderful rock formations. West from the Marbella area, you can easily reach the National Game Reserve near Monda, or the Parque Natural Sierra de Las Nieves, south of Ronda, with its rugged cliffs and great ravines.

Even farther west are the nature parks of Grazalema and Los Alcornocales, both areas of natural, unspoilt landscape. Southeast of Granada and easily accessible from the eastern section of the Costa del Sol is the Parque Natural Sierra Nevada, famed for its striking scenery and diversity of plant and animal life.

Green Tourism
The concept of green tourism is being developed by the regional government of Andalucía. The idea is to create an awareness of the countryside, allowing whole families to observe animals and plants in their natural habitat, enjoy home cooking and have contact with local people. A selection of accommodation offers this type of holiday and information can be obtained from: RAAR (Red Andaluza de Alojamientos Rurales), Apartado 2035, 04080 Almería ☎ 902 44 22 33.
Villas Turísticas, a new project of Turismo Andaluz, consists of groups of tourist villas in parks and remote areas of scenic landscapes. For more information contact: Turismo Andaluz, Calle Compañia, 40, 29008 Málaga, ☎ 952 12 9300

Hiking and Horseriding

The nature parks are wonderful areas for hikers and usually have marked trails for visitors to follow. Information on walking trails can be obtained from local tourist offices. The region of Las Alpujarras with its varied scenery also provides excellent walking terrain.

With its long tradition of raising and riding horses, Andalucía provides an ideal backdrop for long distance trekking. Stables are plentiful and horses can be hired to explore the coast and its hinterland.

Rural Accommodation

Mountain refuges and country houses in traditional Andalucían style make it possible to stay in some of these remote areas. Often located in wild, mountainous terrain and offering magnificent views, they are usually located near access roads.

Birdwatching

Spring and autumn are good periods to watch the European bird migration. Using Spain's southern coast as a resting place, hundreds of species of birds stop here on their journey between Africa and northern Europe. Early morning is a good time to see new arrivals and vantage points are Punta Marroqui at Tarifa, Calahonda, east of Marbella, and Benálmadena.

The nature reserve at the mouth of the river Guadalhorce, located just east of Torremolinos, not far from Málaga airport, is another good place for birdwatching. An area of exceptional beauty, however, is the Laguna de Fuente de Piedra. Located off the N334, west of Antequera, it is known as the Pink Lagoon, after the large colony of pink flamingos which comes here every year to breed. The best time to see these spectacular birds is from the end of January to June.

Las Alpujarras
Lying between the coastal sierras of Lujar, La Contraviesa, Gador and the Sierra Nevada is the region of Las Alpujarras, whose remoteness and inaccessibility has provided a haven to many a fugitive. For the Moors who fled here after the fall of Granada, and the legendary bandits and Republicans who sought refuge here after the civil war, the region has played its role. It now has a growing appeal to expatriates seeking a different sort of retreat.

The cliff-top town of Ronda offers spectacular views of the ravine below and surrounding landscapes

Costa del Sol's Famous

Insired by Granada
The celebrated composer Manuel de Falla lived in Granada for some 20 years, producing great works. American author Washington Irving made his own contribution in propagating the mystique of the area with his collection of tales in *The Alhambra*, written during his stay here in the 1820s.

Writers, Romantics and Travellers

In the 18th and 19th centuries a number of writers, romantics and intrepid travellers discovered for themselves the attractions of Málaga and wrote about it. Hans Christian Andersen, who stayed here towards the middle of the 19th century, wrote of the joyous way of life. Lord Byron, George Borrow and Richard Ford were among others who contributed to discovering Málaga as a winter holiday destination. Later,

the interior of the region attracted writers and poets such as Rainer Maria Rilke, Gerald Brenan, Laurie Lee and Ernest Hemingway. Federico García Lorca, poet and playwright, came from rural Granada.

Art

One of Málaga's most famous sons is the celebrated painter Pablo Ruiz Picasso who was born here in 1881. He began to paint at the age of seven, later joining the School of Fine Arts in La Coruña and moving to Barcelona in 1895. The long-awaited Picasso Museum opened in Málaga in October 2003.

Stars and Celebrities

By the 1960s the tourism industry had developed along the Costa del Sol and the Marbella Club, creation of Alfonso de Hohenlohe, began to attract the rich and famous. Marbella acquired a reputation as a playground for the jet set. Since then the area has seen a flood of personalities, adding their mark to the star-studded scene.

Above right: Lord Byron was an early enthusiast of Málaga
Above: Málaga is justly proud of its famous son Pablo Picasso

The Field of Sport

With its emphasis on sport, it is not surprising that the Costa del Sol receives a fair share of sports personalities. Golfers, Severiano Ballesteros and José Mariá Olazabal are frequent visitors. Tennis stars Bjorn Borg, Arantxa Sanchez Vicario, Conchita Martínez, Boris Becker and Alberto Beresategui visit the area, and former champion Manolo Santana runs a tennis club near Marbella. Other visitors include Ian Botham and David Beckham.

Top Ten

Above: *Patio de Mexuar,
La Alhambra, Granada*
Right: *carving in Vélez-Málaga's
town hall door*

15

1
La Alcazaba, Málaga

🕂 31C2

✉ Calle Alcazabilla, s/n

☎ 952 22 72 30

🕐 Tue–Sun 8:30–7

✋ Inexpensive

🍴 Many near by

🚉 Centro-Alameda railway station

♿ Lift up to Alcazaba, entrance behind the Town Hall (Ayuntamiento)

ℹ Málaga (➤ 29)

The old Moorish fortress or alcazaba, dating back to the second half of the 11th century, stands high above the city of Málaga.

Just up from the Plaza de Aduana are the solid, fortified walls of La Alcazaba, landmark of Málaga. The fortress dates back to the 700s, but most of the structure belongs to the mid-11th century. Entrance is through the gateway known as the Puerta del Cristo (Christ's Door), where the first mass was celebrated following the Christian victory over the town.

The way winds up through attractively laid out gardens and fountains, passing through the gateways of Puerta de las Columnas, Arco del Cristo and Arcos de Granada. Terraces offer magnificent views of the town and harbour. A small palace within the inner perimeter is the home of the Museo de la Alcazaba, which displays a range of Moorish artefacts recovered from the area.

Below the entrance to the Alcazaba are the ruins of a Roman amphitheatre dating back to the second century AD. Parts of the old structure can be seen with restoration continuing. Above the Alcazaba stands the castle which crowns the Gibralfaro Hill (➤ 32).

The cool patios, gardens and fountains of La Alcazaba offer refuge from the heat of the town

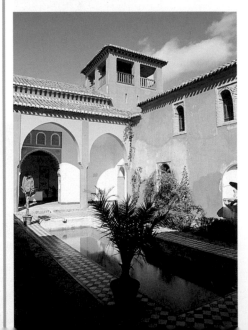

2
La Alhambra, Granada

One of Spain's greatest splendours, the world famous palace of La Alhambra remains as a legacy of the rich culture brought to the peninsula by the Moors.

The Alhambra holds a commanding position above the city of Granada, backed by the snowcapped peaks of the Sierra Nevada. In 1984 it joined UNESCO's list of World Heritage sites. Built by the Moors between the 13th and 15th centuries, it was used as a residence by Muhammad I, and members of the Nasrid dynasty.

Walk up to the entrance from the Plaza Nueva. To the east is the Renaissance palace of Emperor Carlos V, started in 1526 but never completed. To the west stands the Alcazaba, the oldest building on the site. Climb up to the top of the Vela tower for breathtaking views of Granada and the Sierra Nevada.

A tour of the interior of the Casa Real (Royal Palace) reveals the true marvels of the Alhambra: the beautifully decorated Patio de Mexuar, the attractive Patio de los Arrayanes (named after the myrtle trees which line a rectangular pool), and the sumptuous Salón de los Embajadores (Ambassadors' Hall) with its richly carved and coffered ceiling. The Sala de los Abencerrajes has an impressive stalactite ceiling, and the Sala de las Dos Hermanas (Hall of the Two Sisters) features a delicate honeycomb dome. The focal point is the Patio de los Leones (Courtyard of Lions) named after the 12 figures which surround the central fountain.

On the nearby Cerro del Sol (Hill of the Sun) stands the Palacio del Generalife. Dating back to the early 1300s, it was the summer palace of the Moorish kings. The gardens exude an aura of romance, with pools and fountains amidst greenery and flowers.

✚ 47F4

✉ Calle Real, s/n, Granada

☎ 958 02 7900

🕓 Mar–Oct daily 8:30–8. Night visits Tue–Sat, 8:30–6. Fri, Sat 8–9:30. Access to the Palacios Nazaries 8–8:45

✋ Moderate (free for the disabled, senior citizens and Sun after 3PM)

🍴 Few

🚌 Alhambrabus from town centre

♿ Few

❓ Advance booking is strongly recommended. Reservations can be made through any branch of the Banco Bilbao Vizcaya Argentaria (BBV), or by phone on 00 34 915 37 91 78 from outside Spain, or on 902 22 44 60 inside the country. A limited number of tickets are sold daily on site but sell out quickly.

The walls of La Alhambra are bathed in the golden glow of early evening

3
Casares

✚ 46A1

✉ 105km west of Málaga

🍴 Several restaurants

🚌 Local buses

♿ Few

↔ Gaucín (➤ 62)

❓ August Fair (early Aug)

ℹ Tourist information:
Calle Fuente 91,
Casares
☎ 952 89 41 26

With its mass of whitewashed houses sprawling up the hillside, Casares has aquired a reputation for being the most photogenic town in Andalucía.

From whichever angle you approach, the views of Casares are spectacular. The town is easily accessible from the coast: a turning from Estepona leads up into the hills of the Sierra Bermeja. While the drive itself takes you through a scenic route of hills and wooded areas, nothing prepares you for the spectacular view of Casares with its white houses spread over the hill and crowned by an old Moorish castle. Casares saw many battles between the warring Moslems, until it was taken by the Christians in the mid-15th century.

The sight of Casares sprawling over the hillside in a cluster of white houses is always breathtaking

Much of the charm of Casares can be discovered by strolling through its white, terraced streets to the castle above. On the way up, take a look at the 17th-century church of San Sebastian, which contains a statue of the Virgen del Rosario del Campo. The fortress was built in the 13th century on Roman foundations. The 16th-century Church of the Incarnation features a Mudéjar tower.

The views become more spectacular as you make your way up to the summit, where you will be rewarded by a panorama over olive groves, orchards and forests, to the blue of the Mediterranean Sea. Take a look too at the local cemetery, which is beautifully kept and adorned with flowers – not to be missed.

4
Cuevas de Nerja

This series of caverns, close to the coastal town of Nerja, contains spectacular rock formations, and palaeolithic paintings (not open to the public).

✚ 47E2

✉ 4km east of Nerja

☎ 952 52 95 20 (i. Nerja)

🕐 Daily 10–2, 4–6:30

✋ Inexpensive

🍴 Restaurant (££)

🚉 Best by car

♿ None

↔ Nerja (➤ 69)

❓ Summer concerts and ballet performances

ℹ Nerja (➤ 70)

The stunning rock formations found in the Cuevas de Nerja are a big tourist attraction

These limestone caves were discovered by chance in 1959 by a group of boys who were out and about exploring. Beyond the first grotto, great caverns revealed a wonderful world of stalactites and stalagmites, some wall paintings and various items such as stone tools and fragments of pottery. Investigations by experts show that the area must have been inhabited by man over 20,000 years ago. A group of sculptures near the entrance to the caves honours the boys who made the discovery. A small archaeological museum is also located here.

The rock paintings of horses, deer, goats and dolphins are not open for public viewing, but photographs of them are on display, together with some of the artefacts found here. For the tourist, however, the attraction lies in the magnificent display of formations which are enhanced by special lighting effects.

The first chamber provides a magnificent setting for concerts which are held here as part of an annual summer festival. The next cavern is called the Hall of Ghosts after a strange shroud like figure which appears in the stone. Most impressive, however, is the huge Hall of Cataclysms, which features a very tall column rising from a mass of stalactites.

5
La Giralda y La Catedral, Sevilla

42B2

Plaza Virgen de los Reyes

954 21 49 71

Mon–Sat 11–5, Sun 2–6

 Moderate; Sun free

Many restaurants near by

RENFE station

Few

Sevilla (► 81)

The minaret tower known as La Giralda, seen as a symbol of Sevilla, rises proudly above the great Cathedral, third largest in Europe.

The 98m-high brick tower of La Giralda is a prominent feature of Sevilla. It was built in the 12th century as the minaret of the former Great Mosque. In 1565 a section with 25 bells was added and topped with a bronze statue representing Faith, which acts as a *giralda* (weather vane). Climb up to the belfry for magnificent views over the city. There are good views of the town from the first gallery.

The grand cathedral was built in the Gothic style, with some Renaissance influences. The interior is awe-inspiring for its sheer size and the richness of its decoration, with Gothic columns supporting massive arches which reach up to the great heights of the vaulted ceiling.

A handsome 16th-century Plateresque grille in the Sanctuary encloses an immense golden Gothic altarpiece which rates as one of the cathedral's greatest glories and is said to be the largest altar in the world. Started by the Flemish artist Dancart in 1482, it took almost a hundred years to complete the 45 tableaux depicting the life of Jesus and Mary. Above the 16th-century shrine stands an image of the Virgen de la Sede.

The choirstalls are fine examples of flamboyant Gothic. Notable also is the Capilla Real (Royal Chapel). Completed in 1575, it features a richly decorated Renaissance cupola. On either side are the tombs of King Alfonso X (the Wise) and his mother, Beatrice of Swabia. In the south transept lies the ornate tomb of Christopher Columbus, whose body lay here for a time after it was transported from Cuba.

Above: *the Giralda tower is a symbol of Sevilla*

Right: *Sevilla's great Gothic cathedral has a rich interior*

6
Marbella's Casco Antiguo

The jewel of Marbella is its Casco Antiguo (Old Town), a picturesque maze of narrow streets, pretty squares and whitewashed houses.

Located to the north of Avenida Ramón y Cajal, which cuts through the town, Marbella's old quarter is a delightful area in which to browse with its flower-filled streets, neat little houses and small squares. Among its prettiest streets are Remedios, Dolores, Rincón de la Virgen and San Cristóbal which are noted for the brilliance of their flower displays.

Sooner or later everyone converges on the Plaza de los Naranjos, a charming little square lined with neatly pruned orange trees. This is a popular place for a drink or meal out in the open where you can enjoy its lively atmosphere. In the middle of the square is a bust of a serene-looking King Juan Carlos.

✚ 42C1

✉ Marbella (56km west of Malaga)

🍴 Many restaurants (£–£££)

🚌 Marbella bus stop, Avenida Ricardo Soriano 21 (Bus station Avenida del Trapiche s/n ☎ 952 76 44 00)

♿ Few

↔ Remnants of city walls

❓ Pre-Lent Carnival; Feria de San Bernabé (11-18 Jun)

Evidence of its Moorish, Christian and Roman past can be seen on many of its buildings. Take a look at the Iglesia de la Incarnación and, above it, the remaining towers of an old Moorish fortress; the 16th-century Ayuntamiento (Town Hall), Casa Consistorial, which boasts a fine Mudéjar entrance and the Ermita de Nuestro Señor Santiago, Marbella's earliest Christian church. Worth a glimpse, too, is the attractive little Cofradía del Santo Christo de Amor chapel, situated at one end of the Plaza de los Naranjos. A stroll through this area is particularly enjoyable in spring when the heady scent of orange blossom fills the air.

One of the enchanting little streets which form the heart of Marbella's old town

7
La Mezquita, Córdoba

42C3

✉ Torrijos y Cardenal Herrero

☎ 957 47 05 12

🕐 Mon–Sat 10–7, Sun 2–7

✋ Moderate

🍴 Many restaurants near by (£–£££)

🚆 RENFE station, Avenida de America, Córdoba

♿ Few

ℹ Córdoba (➤ 51)

The great mosque of Córdoba is a unique monument which stands as a remarkable achievement of Moorish architecture.

The Mezquita of Córdoba was built in four stages between the 8th and 10th centuries and features amongst the world's largest mosques, remaining as a testimony to the immense power of Islam at the height of its domination of the peninsula.

Do not be discouraged by the mosque's somewhat forbidding outward appearance: its beauty lies within. The main entrance is through the Puerta del Perdón, which leads into the Patio de los Naranjos (Courtyard of the Oranges). Once inside you will be confronted by myriad columns of onyx, marble and granite. The light effects within this dim interior are sensational. The columns are topped by decorated capitals and crowned by the striking red and white arches so characteristic of Moorish architecture. There is a sense of awe and mysticism, special to this particular mosque, which lures the visitor back time and time again.

The striking Moorish interior of Córdoba's fabled mosque is seen as one of Andalucía's richest jewels

To find a Christian cathedral within the very heart of the mosque comes as something of a surprise. It was built in the 1520s on the orders of Hapsburg Emperor Carlos V, who later regretted his decision. However, it does manage to blend fairly well into its surroundings.

Rising above the Puerta del Perdón is the bell tower, which offers splendid views.

8
Mijas

With its attractive mountain setting, picturesque little streets and whitewashed houses, Mijas is a popular excursion from the coast.

Despite the fact that Mijas caters so obviously for the tourist it has still managed to retain its charm. The little town is undeniably picturesque, with its white houses, narrow winding streets, flowers and plants. The setting is most attractive, offering magnificent views of the pine-clad mountains which surround it and the coast below. Furthermore, its proximity to the coast, a drive of some 20 minutes or so, makes it an ideal destination for a day's excursion.

On the central square of Plaza de la Virgen you will see the over-patient donkeys lined up. Adorned with colourful saddles and tassles, they can be hired for rides around town, serving as donkey taxis. Concerts and fiestas are sometimes held in the square, which centres around a small fountain and is a popular meeting place. Below is a large parking lot, which has greatly helped to ease traffic problems.

Adjoining the square is a neat little park with fine views. Hollowed out from a chunk of rock is a delightful little chapel known as the Santuario de la Virgen de la Peña Limosnas. Inside is the image of Santa Maria de la Peña, along with some impressive candlesticks, embroidered garments and other religious relics.

A stroll to the Plaza de la Constitución leads past the Miniature Museum 'Carromato de Max', which has a collection of tiny curios. Up the slope from the Plaza stands the charming little parish church of La Inmaculada Concepción, built mostly in the Mozarabic style. Near by is the town's small, rectangular bullring.

➕ 46C2

✉ 37km west of Málaga

🍴 Many restaurants (£–£££)

🚌 Local bus services

♿ Few

↔ Benalmádena Pueblo (► 47)

❓ St Anthony's Day (16–17 Jan); Feria de la Virgen de la Peña (early Sep); Romería de Santa Teresa (end Oct)

ℹ Tourist information: Ayuntamiento, Plaza Virgen de la Peña s/n ☎ 952 48 59 00

The picturesque little mountain town of Mijas

9
Puerto Banús

 46B1

 64km west of Málaga, 6km west of Marbella

 Many bars and restaurants (££–£££)

 Bus services from Marbella and San Pedro de Alcántara

Few

San Pedro de Alcántara (➤ 78)

 Regattas, sailing and fishing competitions

 Tourist Information: Avenida Principal s/n ☎ 952 11 38 30 (summer only)

The dazzling marina of Puerto Banús, with its luxurious yachts, trendy restaurants and bars, serves as a magnet for visitors to the Costa del Sol.

A stay on the Costa del Sol would be incomplete without a visit to Puerto Banús, one of the Costa's most famous attractions. Built in 1968, Puerto José Banús, as it is also known, was the creation of promoter José Banús and was one of Spain's first village-type harbour developments. The result is most attractive and worth a visit.

Backed by the mountains, a ring of brilliant white apartment houses surrounds the marina, which is filled with craft of all sizes, from mega yachts to small sailing

Above: *enjoying a drink in lively Puerto Banús*

Right: *the yacht-filled harbour of Puerto Banús presents a glamorous scene*

boats. A feature of Banús is the Arab-built complex of luxury apartments, located on the right as you enter the port. With its opulent marble façade and gleaming turrets, the inspiration could have been taken straight from the *Arabian Nights*.

Around the port is a string of cafés, bars and restaurants, along with boutiques and gift shops. While frontline restaurants are *the* places in which to be seen, better value is sometimes found in some of the small restaurants in the streets behind, tucked away up flights of stairs. In season the quayside is thronged with people who come to see, or to be seen – this can be a great place for celebrity-spotting. The Saladuba Pub and the Frank Sinatra Bar are favourite haunts for indulging this particular pastime.

At night the place becomes a hive of activity, as the smart restaurants, trendy piano bars and clubs fill up with beautiful people. While the glamour of its earlier days may have dimmed, Banús still rates as a star attraction.

10
Ronda's Puente Nuevo

 46A2

✉ 118km northwest of Málaga

🍴 Many restaurants in Ronda (£–£££)

🚌 Buses from Algeciras, Cádiz, Málaga (via Torremolinos, Marbella, San Pedro) and Servilla

↔ Ronda (➤ 74), Cuevas de la Pileta (➤ 75)

ℹ Ronda (➤ 74)

The Puente Nuevo spans the deep Tajo gorge, linking the old Ronda with the 'new town'

The old town of Ronda is famed for its spectacular setting and views of the bridge over the El Tajo ravine.

Ronda has long associations with painters and writers, for many of whom the town has held a deep fascination. The scene of Ronda perched on the clifftop and, in particular, the bridge which spans the gorge, has been the subject of countless paintings and photographs.

Ronda is one of Spain's oldest cities. Situated within the rugged landscape of the Serranía de Ronda, the town is split in two, divided by the gorge of the River Guadalevín, which is spanned by the Puente Nuevo (New Bridge). The dramatic views from the bridge, combined with the attractions of the old town and its historical interest, make Ronda (➤ 74) a top excursion for visitors staying along the coast.

The Puente Nuevo (which has become the city's symbol) was begun in 1751 and completed in 1793. It stands a full 96m above the Tajo gorge at its highest and narrowest point. The unfortunate architect fell to his death from a basket lowered to allow him to inspect the building work.

What To See

Above: Alcazár gardens, Córdoba
Right: sculpture, Torremolinos

Málaga

Málaga is the second city of Andalucía and capital of the Costa del Sol, forming a natural divide between its western and eastern sections. The town has an attractive setting, crowned by the old Moorish castle which stands atop the Gibralfaro Hill, holding a commanding view of Málaga's harbour and the wide sweep of the bay.

The backing of the Montes de Málaga mountain range provides shelter from the wind, ensuring a pleasant Mediterranean climate which is particularly agreeable from autumn through to spring.

To many tourists Málaga has tended to serve primarily as a gateway to the coast or its hinterland. Now, with the opening of the Picasso Museum, along with several other new museums and expansion projects, there is an awakening of interest in the city whose old quarters, churches, traditional bars and restaurants exude a true flavour of Andalucía.

'The people all looked in a good humour...They gave me a feeling of joy and exhilaration. O Málaga, glorious city, here shall I be at home!'

HANS CHRISTIAN ANDERSEN
A Visit to Spain (1862)

Málaga

Málaga has, by and large, retained its own personality over the years, remaining relatively untouched by the tourist boom along the coast.

It is well worth spending some time to explore the town. Off the Alameda Principal, Málaga's main avenue, attractively shaded by palms and lined with flower stalls and kiosks, is the old town. Here you will find yourself in another world of narrow streets with traditional bars and bodegas exuding a decidedly local flavour.

Málaga's outstanding features are the old Moorish Alcazaba (► 16) and the Castillo de Gibralfaro (► 32), which offer magnificent views of the town and the bay. Other attractions include the cathedral, the Museo Picasso, the Museo de Artes y Costumbres Populares and the Palacio de la Aduana. Among the many small churches do not miss the chapel of the Santuario de la Victoria. For good seafood restaurants head for the beach suburbs of El Palo or Pedregalejo.

A good way to visit the town is by the electric train which runs half hourly between Fuengirola and Málaga, making stops at Torremolinos and other centres en route.

The Gibralfaro castle offers a panoramic view of Málaga town, with the harbour and coastline beyond

🛈 Tourist information:
   Pasaje de Chinitas 4
   ☎ 952 21 34 45

What to See in Málaga

CASA NATAL DE PICASSO ⭐

Spain's celebrated painter, Pablo Ruiz Picasso, was born in 1881 in the corner house of an elegant yellow-toned block on Plaza de la Merced. His birthplace was declared an historic-artistic monument in 1983, and in 1991 it became the headquarters of the Pablo Ruiz Picasso Foundation. The centre has been created to foster cultural activities, including the promotion of contemporary art with a special emphasis on Picasso himself.

Visitors are welcome to take a look around the small area on the first floor where you can see a few photographs, memorabilia and documentation relating to Picasso's life, in addition to works by other artists.

It was here that Picasso began to paint, helped by his father, an art teacher, who had recognised his young son's talent.

➕ 31C2
✉ Plaza de la Merced 15
☎ 952 06 02 15
🕐 Mon–Sat 10–8, Sun 10–2
🍴 Free
🍴 Many near by (£–£££)
🚉 Centro-Alameda railway station
♿ Few

Palacio de la Aduana

The Hall of Columns (Salón de Columnas), in this neo-classical former Customs House, which was on the waterfront until the construction of the Paseo del Parque, now exhibits parts of the art collection from the Museum of Fine Arts (Museo de Bellas Artes). The exhibitions and displays are changed at regular intervals. Eventually the whole collection will be re-housed in a new Palace of Fine Arts.
☎ 952 21 36 80

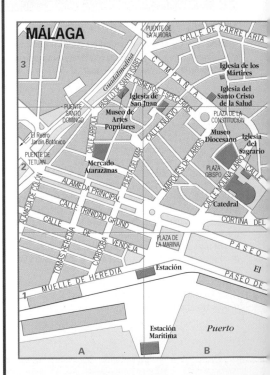

The site of Málaga's Gibralfaro castle was once occupied by a lighthouse which served to guide the ships into the harbour

+ 31D1
⊠ Lighthouse Hill
☎ 952 22 72 30
🕐 Daily 9–6
👎 Inexpensive
🍴 Parador near by
🚌 35
♿ None

CASTILLO DE GIBRALFARO ✪✪

Right above the Alcazaba stands the Castillo de Gibralfaro, crowning the hill of the same name. It was built by Yusef I of Granada at the beginning of the 14th century on a formerly Phoenician site and lighthouse from which its name was derived – *gebel-faro* (rock of the lighthouse) signifies the beacon that served to guide ships into the harbour.

This was once the scene of a three-month siege by the citizens of Málaga against the Catholic monarchs Ferdinand and Isabella. The matter was concluded only when hunger led to capitulation, after which Ferdinand occupied the site while his queen took up residence in the town. All that remains today of this historic monument is a series of solid ramparts which rise majestically among dense woods of pines and eucalyptus, with the Alcazaba not far below.

Although it can be reached on foot from the Alcazaba, it's a safer bet to visit the castle direct, by bus, car, even by horse and carriage. You can round off a visit with a cool drink at the nearby Parador de Málaga which also offers panoramic views of the city and harbour, with landmarks such as the cathedral and bullring clearly visible.

The energetic can take a walk up the Gibralfaro Hill to the castle, which stands above the Alcazaba

Left: *the solitary steeple of Málaga's cathedral*

Below: *fine carving on the choir stalls in the cathedral*

CATEDRAL ✪✪

Málaga's cathedral is large and has a somewhat sombre exterior. It was built between 1528 and 1782 on or near the site of a former mosque. While original plans had allowed for two towers, lack of funds resulted in the completion of only one, giving rise to the name by which the cathedral is affectionately referred to, La Manquita, loosely interpreted as 'the little one-armed woman'.

The interior has influences of the Renaissance and baroque styles. The notable 17th-century choir stalls of mahogany and cedarwood were designed by Luis Ortíz. After his death the 40 finely carved statues of the saints behind each stall were completed by Pedro de Mena, one of Spain's most celebrated wood-carvers of the time, who spent some years in Málaga. Some of the chapels leading off the aisles also contain works by Pedro de Mena and his tutor Alonso Cano.

Adjoining the cathedral is the Iglesia del Sagrario. Founded in the 15th century on the site of a mosque, the church has an unusual rectangular shape. Its Isabelline-Gothic portal is the only remaining part of the original structure, which was rebuilt in 1714. The interior is richly decorated and its main altar features a magnificent 16th-century retable.

➕ 30B2
🅾 Calle Molina Larios, s/n
☎ 952 21 59 17
🕐 Mon–Sat 10–6:45
💷 Inexpensive
🍴 None
🚉 Centro-Alameda railway station
♿ Few

30A2

Huge choice of
restaurants (£–£££)

Above: *Málaga's harbour
bustling with activity*

Below: *Málaga's old
narrow streets can lead
to many a surprise*

CENTRO (CENTRE) ★

The heart of Málaga is found north of the Alameda
Principal, Málaga's main avenue, and east of the Río
Guadalmedina, which separates the old town from the
new. As soon as you turn off the Alameda you will enter a
labyrinthine medieval world of narrow, twisting roads.
There is much to be enjoyed here, increasingly so the
more you find your bearings. The centre is small and many
streets are pedestrianised, so that exploring on foot is both
enjoyable and viable.

Another way in which to enjoy a little tour around town
is by horse-drawn carriage, a good option if you are tired or
feeling the heat. You will see these lined up by the
cathedral, in the Paseo del Parque and various other points
around the town.

While the cathedral is a focal point from which to start
exploring, the main artery of the city centre is the busy
shopping street, Calle Marqués de Larios, which leads
from the Alameda Principal north to the Plaza de la
Constitución. On either side are old, narrow streets,
alleyways and tiny squares where you can happily browse
for hours. Within this area are a number of churches and a
few museums, all within close range. You will also
discover some delightfully picturesque little streets lined
with gaily coloured houses and shops.

Málaga is famed for its *tapas* bars. For some local
atmosphere try one of the so-called *rutas del tapeo* (*tapas*
route) which cover the area west of Calle Marqués de
Larios, centering around Calle Nueva.

A Walk Through the Old Town

This walk starts in the Plaza de la Marina and makes a tour of Málaga's old quarters, taking in the cathedral and several churches.

From Plaza de la Marina take Calle Molina Lario, left of the Málaga Palacio Hotel which faces you. A few moments' walk will bring you right up to the cathedral.

Horses and carriages line up here ready to take visitors on a tour around the town. Opposite, on the Plaza Obispo, is the old Palacio Episcopal, which contains some delightful 'hidden' patios and has exhibitions of contemporary art.

Turn right along Calle Santa Maria and take Calle San Agustín.

On your right is the Palacio Buenavista, which now houses the new Museo Picasso. You will now enter an attractive section of pedestrianised streets and pretty coloured houses.

Take a right fork into Calle Granada which takes you by the Iglesia de Santiago. From here continue to the Plaza de la Merced.

The centre of the Plaza de la Merced is marked by an obelisk in memory of General Torrijos and his men who were shot after the War of Independence. On the far corner, in an attractive block of houses, is the Casa Natal de Picasso, birthplace of Pablo Picasso, now centre of the Picasso Foundation.

Return down Calle Granada to Plaza del Siglo and on to the Plaza de la Constitución, then stroll down Calle Marqués Larios, Málaga's main shopping street. Down on the left make a short detour through the archway and along Pasaje de Chinitas, which leads to a tiny square. Complete the walk down Calle Larios and turn into the Alameda Principal to Plaza de la Marina.

Distance
4km

Time
3–4 hours, depending on visits to churches

Start/end point
Plaza de la Marina
✚ 30B1

Lunch
Espartero (££)
✉ Esparteros 4
☎ 952 60 30 22

The statue of Santa Maria de la Victoria

The Iglesia de los Mártires
(Church of the Martyrs)
has a fine Mudéjar tower

Iglesias (Churches)

When strolling about Málaga's old town, you are more than likely to pass by several, if not all, of the following churches. Take time to have a look inside, as each has its own individual attraction. With the exception of the Santuario de la Victoria, which is slightly away from the centre, all are within easy walking distance of each other.

CATEDRAL (▶ 33)

IGLESIA DE LOS MÁRTIRES

The church was founded in 1487 by the Catholic Monarchs and dedicated to the martyrs of the town. It features a striking Mudéjar tower which was added later and a richly decorated baroque-style interior, which includes a notable sculpture by Francisco Ortíz of Jesus praying on the Mount of Olives.

✝ 30B3
✉ Plaza Mártires
☎ 952 21 27 24
🕐 Daily 10–2:30, 6–7…30
👋 Free
♿ Few

IGLESIA DE SANTIAGO

Founded in 1490, the church is noted for its tall, Mudéjar-style steeple and baroque interior which contains some notable chapels. Pablo Picasso's baptismal certificate is stored here.

✝ 31C2
✉ Calle Granada 62
☎ 952 21 03 99
🕐 Daily 9–1:30, 6–9

IGLESIA DEL SANTO CRISTO DE LA SALUD

The interior of this 17th-century church is a real gem. Note the brilliant altarpiece and beautifully decorated cupola. The church also contains the tomb of architect Pedro de la Mena.

✝ 30B3
✉ Calle Compania
☎ 952 21 34 56

IGLESIA SAN JUAN BAUTISTA

Founded in 1490, the church's baroque-style tower above the main entrance was added in 1770. Inside are several fine chapels and a rich altarpiece. The 17th-century figure of San Juan is the work of Francisco Ortíz.

✝ 30B3
✉ Calle San Juan, 3
☎ 952 21 12 83
🕐 Daily 8:30–1, 6–8

SANTUARIO DE LA VICTORIA

The church was erected in 1487 on the site where the Catholic Monarchs pitched their tents during the siege of that year. A major feature is the magnificent retable which rises above the main altar. High up, amidst a flourish of exuberant ornamentation, is a small *camerín* (chapel) containing a statue of the Madonna and Child (reached by stairs at the far end of the church). In the crypt is the family vault of the counts of Buenavista, who were responsible for the rebuilding of the church in the 17th century.

✝ Off map 31D2
✉ Plaza del Santuario
☎ 952 25 26 47
🕐 Tue–Fri 10–12, 4:30–7, Sat 10–12
👋 Free
🚊 Centro-Alameda railway station
♿ Few

MUSEO DE ARTES Y COSTUMBRES POPULARES ⭐⭐

This charming little museum is housed in the Mesón de la Victoria, a former 17th-century inn, now attractively restored. The museum is on two floors and was created to give an insight into the past ways and customs of the people of the region.

The first rooms, which display agricultural items, open out onto an attractive courtyard with tropical plants. In the rooms beyond you can see a fishing boat and some

+ 30A3
✉ Passillo de Santa Isabel 10
☎ 952 21 71 37
🕐 Mon–Sat 10–1, 5–7
👛 Inexpensive
♿ Few
🚉 Railway station Centro-Alameda

interiors of old houses. Upstairs displays include collections of costumes, ceramics and tiles, fascinating old posters announcing fiestas, religious items and an enchanting little group of clay figures depicting a *panda de verdiales* (group of regional musicians).

Above: leafy courtyard of the Museo de Artes Populares

MUSEO PICASSO ⭐⭐

The new Picasso Museum is installed in the Palacio Buenavista, former home of the Palace of Fine Arts. The museum contains over 180 works by the artist, including drawings, engravings, lithographs, sculptures and ceramics, the majority of which have been donated by Christina, Picasso's daughter-in-law. Work continues to extend the premises and restore the façade. The museum opened in 2003.

+ 31C1
✉ Palacio de Buenavista, Calle San Augustin, 8
☎ 902 44 33 77
🕐 Tue–Thu 10–8, Fri and Sat 10–1:30
👛 Moderate
♿ Wheelchairs available upon request

Left: one of the Museo de Artes Populares' old 'Grandes Fiestas' posters

Parques y Jardines (Parks & Gardens)

In and around Málaga are several attractive parks and gardens, of which the following are outstanding.

EL PARQUE

Malaga's city park, which runs alongside the Paseo del Parque, was created at the end of the 19th century making use of land reclaimed from the sea. The park contains beautiful tropical flowering trees and shrubs. Many of the unusual and exotic species to be seen here were brought from overseas when Málaga was an important world trading centre.

EL RETIRO JARDÍN BOTÁNICO-ORNITOLÓGICO

The El Retiro Park is an old botanic garden and bird sanctuary, where monks once came to find peace and to meditate. Recently opened to the public, its ornithological park contains hundreds of birds, many of them endangered species. A peaceful stroll can be enjoyed amongst its trees, ponds and fountains.

JARDÍN BOTÁNICO-HISTÓRICO
'LA CONCEPCIÓN'

Just outside Málaga, Finca de la Concepción is another magnificent botanic garden. You can follow a marked path through exotic trees and plants, passing Roman sculpture and a waterfall.

Sidebar (El Parque):
- ✚ 30B1/31C1
- ✉ Between Paseo del Parque and Paseo de Espana
- ☎ None
- ⏰ Daily
- 💶 Free
- ♿ Good

Sidebar (El Retiro):
- ✚ Off map 30A2
- ✉ Ctra de Coin
- ☎ 952 62 16 00
- ⏰ Daily 9–6
- 💶 Moderate
- 🍴 Restaurant (££)
- ♿ Few

Sidebar (La Concepción):
- ✚ 46C2
- ✉ Along the N331 to Antequera, just off the Málaga ring road
- ☎ 952 25 21 48
- ⏰ Tue–Sun 10–4:30
- 💶 Inexpensive
- ♿ Few

The Paseo del Parque offers a delightful stroll amidst shady trees, fountains and colourful tropical plants

A Walk Around the Churches & Museums of Málaga

This is a leisurely walk which includes Málaga's main market, an attractive little museum and several churches.

From the Centro–Alameda take the Alameda Principal exit. Cross over at the traffic lights and turn into Calle Torregarda to the Mercado de Atarazas, Malaga's main market.

Pass through the market to take a look at the colourful displays of fruit and vegetables and, in particular, the wonderful selection of glistening fresh fish.

Emerge into Plaza de Arriola and continue along the Paseo Santa Isabel.

You will find yourself on the banks of the dried up Río Guadalmedina. Look out for a flight of steps on your right which leads down through a tiny garden to the Museo de Artes Populares.

Continue along the Paseo Santa Isabel and turn right down Calle Cisneros.

This brings you into a picturesque part of the old town where a right turn down a narrow alleyway leads to the Iglesia San Juan, standing on a small square.

Retrace your steps, turn right onto Calle Especerías, left along Calle Salvago, left again and right to Plaza San Ignacio.

Take a look at the Iglesia del Corazón de Jesús. Turn back and take the Calle de los Mártires. On the small square which follows you cannot miss the striking Mudéjar tower of the Iglesia de los Mártires.

Return and turn left along Calle Compañia, past the Iglesia de Santo Cristo de la Salud.

Wander through the Plaza de la Constitución and take the Calle Nueva into the heart of Malaga's famous area for *tapas* bars. Some refreshments will no doubt be welcome here. The Calle Puerta del Mar leads straight down to the Alameda Principal and back to the station.

Distance
3.5km

Time
3–4 hours, depending on visits

Start/end point
Railway station Centro-Alameda
✚ 30B1

Lunch
Mesón la Aldea (£)
✉ Esparteros, 5
☎ 952 22 76 89

A stroll in the old quarters of the town will take you by some colourful old façades

Costa del Sol & Beyond

The Costa del Sol falls into two parts with Málaga forming the divide between the western and eastern sections. The most developed and best known area is west of Málaga, starting with Torremolinos and including the major resorts of Benalmádena Costa, Fuengirola, Marbella and Estepona. This part of the coastline is virtually one long stream of apartment blocks, marina developments, hotels and restaurants. The eastern Costa del Sol, stretching towards Almería, has a totally different appeal. The coastline is often broken up by rocks and small coves and is much less developed, with Nerja standing out as a favoured resort. The interior offers excursions to delightful white Andalucían villages nestling in the mountains, and to the great historic cities of Granada, Córdoba and Sevilla.

> *' The road to Málaga*
> *followed a beautiful but*
> *exhausted shore, seemingly*
> *forgotten by the world.*
> *I remember the names –*
> *San Pedro, Estepona,*
> *Marbella and Fuengirola… '*

LAURIE LEE
As I Walked Out One Midsummer
Morning 1939

———————•———————

Left: *taking a break outside the Mezquita in Córdoba*

41

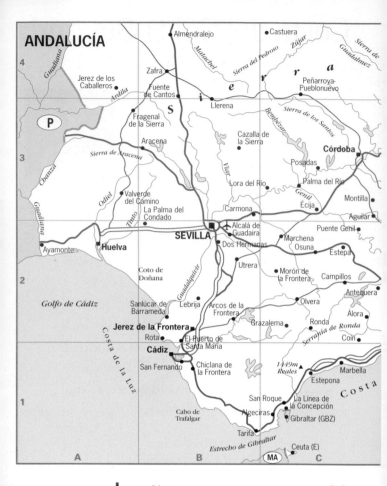

ANDALUCÍA

Alméndralejo • Castuera

Jerez de los Caballeros

Zafra

Fuente de Cantos

Fragenal de la Sierra

Aracena

Peñarroya-Pueblonuevo

Llerena

Cazalla de la Sierra

Córdoba

Sierra de Aracena

Posadas

Lora del Rio

Palma del Rio

Valverde del Camino

La Palma del Condado

Carmona

Écija

Montilla

Aguilar

Alcalá de Guadaira

Puente Genil

SEVILLA

Dos Hermanas

Marchena

Osuna

Estepa

Huelva

Ayamonte

Coto de Doñana

Utrera

Morón de la Frontera

Campillos

Antequera

Golfo de Cádiz

Sanlúcar de Barrameda

Lebrija

Arcos de la Frontera

Olvera

Álora

Jerez de la Frontera

Rota

El Puerto de Santa María

Grazalema

Ronda

Coín

Cádiz

San Fernando

Chiclana de la Frontera

1449m Reales

Marbella

Estepona

San Roque

La Línea de la Concepción

Cabo de Trafalgar

Algeciras

Gibraltar (GBZ)

Tarifa

Estrecho de Gibraltar

Ceuta (E)

MA

Costa de la Luz

Guadiana
Ardila
Chanza
Odiel
Tinto
Guadalquivir
Viar
Genil
Bembézar
Sierra de los Santos
Ziújar
Sierra de Guadalmez
Serranía de Ronda
Costa

ALMUÑÉCAR ⚫⚫

✚ 47F2
✉ 84km east of Málaga
🍴 Variety of restaurants
🚌 Local bus services
♿ Few
ℹ Tourist Information:
Avenida Europa-
Palacete La Najarra
☎ 958 63 11 25

Almuñécar, situated in the province of Granada, within the coastline now designated as the Costa Tropical, lies amidst orchards of tropical fruits. It presents a very picturesque scene, typical of so many villages to be found in southern Spain, with a cluster of whitewashed houses rising up the hillside, crowned by an old castle. Its history goes back to the time of the Phoenicians, with subsequent occupation by the Romans and the Moors.

The Castillo de San Miguel stands on top of a tall rock, dividing two bays. It was built during the reign of Carlos V, over the site of a former Moorish fortress, and features a great square tower known as La Mazmorra.

The town itself is a delightful jumble of narrow, cobble-stoned streets, climbing steeply up to the summit. Do not

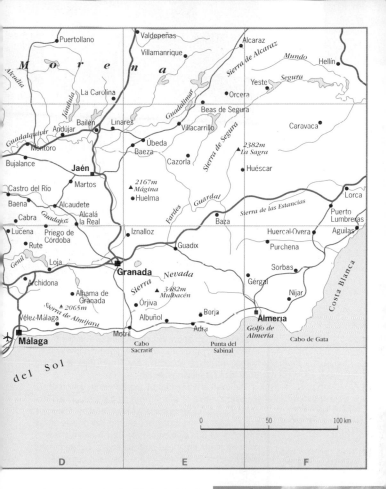

miss a visit to the Ornithological Park located at the foot of the hill. Here you can see brilliantly coloured parrots and rare species of birds in a beautiful setting of subtropical plants and flowers. The seafront is lined with apartment blocks, bars and restaurants, with a lively scene by day and night, during the season.

Also worth a visit is the small archaeological museum housed in the Cueva de los Siete Palacios, thought to have been a Roman reservoir for water. The museum has a display of artefacts from the area (🕐 Tue–Sat 11–2 and 6–8).

A look-out post at nearby Punta de la Mona offers sweeping views of the harbour and the Mediterranean.

Almuñécar is one of the most prominent resort towns along the coast east of Málaga

43

Well worth a visit is Antequera, an interesting old town with many churches, convents and squares

🚩 46C3
✉ 54km north of Málaga
🍴 Good choice of restaurants (£–£££)
🚌 From Málaga
🚆 From Málaga
♿ Few
❓ Feria de Primavera (31 May–1/2 Jun); Noche Flamenca de Santa Maria (end Jul); August Fair (early Aug)
ℹ Tourist Information: Plaza San Sebastian 7 ☎ 952 70 25 05

Dólmen de Menga
✉ 1km east of Antequera
🕐 Wed–Sat 9–6, Tue, Sun 9–3:30
🖐 Free
🚌 From Antequera
🚆 From Antequera
♿ None

ANTEQUERA ★★

Antequera is known for its convents, churches and elegant mansions, which show various architectural influences. It is easily reached by means of the good motorway from Málaga and can be visited in a day. (Town Walk ➤ 45 and Drive from Torremolinos ➤ 88.)

The town is dominated by the old castle, which offers excellent views of the surrounding plains. The 16th-century church of Santa María la Mayor, near by, features a fine Mudéjar ceiling. Dominant are the bell towers of the churches of San Sebastian and San Augustín, which combine the Mudéjar and baroque styles. Outstanding is the church of El Carmen, which has been designated a national monument. Formerly a convent, it is noted for its rich interior and impressive wooden altar.

The discovery of prehistoric tombs in nearby caves has given the town added importance. Of the three caves here, the most important is the **Dólmen de Menga**. Its large cavern contains a series of stones and columns which support huge slabs that form the roof, believed to date back to circa 2500 BC.

The Parque Nacional El Torcal de Antequera is located some 16km south of Antequera and covers an extended area of grey limestone rocks and boulders which have been weathered with time to form the most weird and wonderful shapes. There is a small information office by the car park and a magnificent view from the nearby Mirador el Ventanillo. Several walking trails among the boulders are marked by arrows (yellow for a shorter walk, red for a longer one).

A Stroll Around Antequera's Churches & Mansions

This walk takes in some of Antequera's many churches and includes magnificent views. Most churches close from 1:30 to 4PM so a morning walk is recommended. On the Plaza San Sebastian look at the 16th-century Colegiata de San Sebastian. Walk up Calle Infante Don Fernando. Take a look at the Iglesia de San Agustín, on the left, and further along, on the right, you will pass the Palacio Consistorial (Town Hall) and the Convento de los Remedios.

Just past the Iglesia de San Juan de Dios turn sharp right into Calle Cantareros and back towards the centre.

You will pass the house of the Condado de Colchado and the Convento de la Madre de Dios de Monteagudo.

Continue down Calle Diego Ponce, then turn left up to Plaza San Francisco and the Plazuela de San Zoilo.

This brings you to the Convento Real de San Zoilo, one of Antequera's National Monuments, and some fine views.

Take Calle Calzada and continue up Cuesta de Los Rojos to Plaza del Carmen. On Calle del Carmen is the Iglesia del Carmen. Return and take a sharp right, turn up Calle del Colegio, a very steep climb, to the Arco de los Gigantes (Arch of Giants) on your left.

Pass through the arch to the Real Colegiata de Santa María la Mayor. Near by are the Roman Baths.

Return through the Arch and go left along Calle Herradores to the charming Plaza del Portichuelo on which stands the Iglesia de Santa María de Jesús.

Distance
4.5km

Time
About 3 hours

Start point
Plaza San Sebastian
🚶 46C3

End point
Plaza del Portichuelo
🚶 46C3

Lunch
Restaurante El Angelote (££)
✉ Calle Encarnación
(Esquina Cosa Viejo)
☎ 952 70 34 65

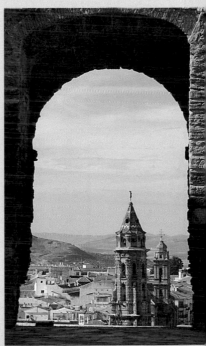

Antequera's rooftops seen through the castle's archway

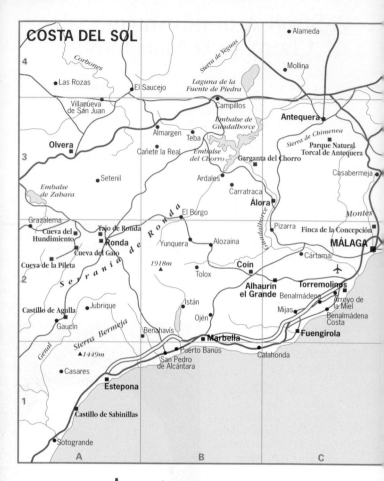

COSTA DEL SOL

BENALMÁDENA COSTA ★

Benalmádena Costa is, in effect, a natural extension of Torremolinos, taking over where Torremolinos leaves off. It covers a long stretch of coast lined with the type of high-rise apartment blocks which characterise this section of the Costa del Sol, along with a string of restaurants, cafés, bars and shops. An attractive seafront promenade makes it possible to walk from Torremolinos all the way along the coast to Benalmádena's Puerto Marina (► 48) – you need time and energy for this!

The area has been noticeably upgraded in recent years, partly due to the Casino and the 18-hole Torrequebrada golf course, located a short distance up into the hills. There are also facilities for waterskiing, jetskiing, windsurfing, sailing and all the popular watersports.

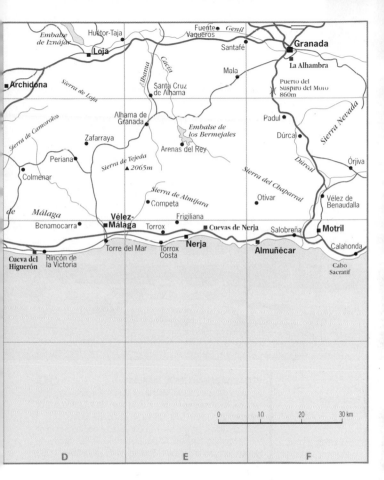

Map scale: 0 — 10 — 20 — 30 km

Grid references: D, E, F

BENALMÁDENA PUEBLO ⭐⭐

Two small inland communities present a complete contrast to the attractions on the coastal strip of Benalmádena Costa. About 1km into the hills is Arroyo de la Miel which has developed into quite a lively centre with modern housing, shops and restaurants. Just up the road is the Tivoli World Show and Amusement Park.

Further up the hill is Benalmádena Pueblo whose origins are thought to date back to Phoenician times. This is a charming little village of narrow twisting streets and whitewashed houses. With attractive views of the coast and surrounding landscapes, it offers a rural atmosphere. The Museo Arqueológico contains some pre-Columbian exhibits, along with artefacts from Roman and early Iberian times.

🚩 46C2

✉ 3km west of Arroyo de la Miel

🍴 Variety of restaurants and bars

♿ Few

🔁 Tivoli World Amusement Park (➤ 106)

❓ Local fair (15 Aug); Feria de San Juan (24 Jun) at Arroyo de la Miel

Benalmádena's Puerto Marina offers a variety of attractions to suit visitors of all ages

➕ 46C2
✉ Benalmádena Costa
🍴 Variety of restaurants, bars and pubs
♿ Few
↔ Torrequebrada development with casino, nightclub and golf course (▶ 108)

BENALMÁDENA PUERTO MARINA ✪✪

Benalmádena's Puerto Marina, or Puerto Departivo as it is known, has developed into one of the most prominent of the marinas which have sprung up along the coast.

Built initially as a small harbour surrounded by a ring of whitewashed houses, Andalucian-style, it has gradually grown into an impressive marina, with more than 1,000 berths. Numerous shops, open-air bars and restaurants line the quayside. A centrepiece is provided by a complex of luxurious apartments called Las Islas de Puerto Marina. Constructed in flamboyant style, they do appear like islands floating on the water.

The marina offers a good outing to suit all age groups. An outstanding attraction is Sea Life Benalmádena, which can be enjoyed by the whole family, while another popular venue is the *Willow*, the Mississippi-style paddleboat; moored here permanently, it is fitted out as a restaurant and nightclub.

With its open-air cafés, restaurants and shops, Puerto Marina continues to increase in popularity, especially at weekends, attracting Spaniards and visitors alike with further expansion planned. An ultra-modern underwater lighting system, installed in the waters of the harbour, creates a magical effect at night.

Up Into the Hills to Mijas

This drive takes you up into the hills through attractive scenery to the picturesque little town of Mijas, passing a couple of other typical Andalucían villages on the return to the coast.

From Benalmádena Costa take the N340 east for a short distance. Turn inland, following the sign to Arroyo de la Miel. In the village turn left at the traffic lights and follow the signs to Tivoli World. Continue up the hill and pass by the Tivoli World Amusement Park on your right to Benalmádena Pueblo. Proceed through the village and follow the signs to Mijas.

A very winding road (with some bad stretches and narrow sections) takes you through lovely pine-clad hills, with fine views down to the coast. You should reach Mijas some 45 minutes later. Take time to explore this delightful little town, noted for its setting in the hills.

Take the A387 northwest to Alhaurín el Grande, 17km on.

Drive on through a winding stretch of reddish rocks and pines, with some fine panoramic views on your left and bear right, continuing on the A387, to the village of Alhaurín el Grande. Look for the signs and join the A366 northwest to Coín, which you should reach some 10 minutes later.

After Coín, turn onto the A355, following the signs for Ojén–Marbella, to Monda. Continue on the A355 which now heads south towards Ojén–Marbella.

The road from here to Ojén has a good surface and continuing curves as it passes through an area of rocks and wooded hills. It will take you some 45 minutes to reach Ojén.

Continue south for 8km to the coastal road. Join the N340 and take direction Málaga back to Benalmádena Costa.

Distance
116km

Time
About 5 hours, allowing time to visit Mijas

Start/end point
Banalmádena Costa
✠ 46C2

Lunch
Restaurante Mesón El Olivar (££)
✉ Avenida Virgon de la Pena (edif. El Roasrio)
☎ 952 48 61 96
🕐 Closed Sat and Feb

Drive up into the hills to the quiet little village of Ojén

CASARES (► 18, TOP TEN)

CÓMPETA ✪

Way up in the mountains of La Axarquia, the region east of Málaga, is the small town of Cómpeta, which can be reached by taking the road leading inland from Torox-Costa.

Cómpeta is noted for its attractive setting, perched atop a mountain ridge surrounded by vineyards. It is one of a number of easily accessible Andalucían towns and villages located in the hills which offer fine views down to the coast. The town is made up of a cluster of whitewashed houses and winding streets. On the main square stands the baroque Iglesia de la Asunción, which features an impressive bell tower.

Cómpeta has quite a sizeable community of foreign residents, a number of whom are involved with craft industries. A big attraction is the lively wine festival which is held each year in August in the main square.

🟥 47E3
✉ 51km east of Málaga
🍴 Several restaurants (£–££)
🚻 Local services
♿ Few
🔁 Nerja (► 69)
❓ Noche del Vino (15 Aug)
ℹ Tourist information: Plaza Almijira s/n ☎ 952 55 33 01

Left and below: different aspects of the typically Andalucian village of Cómpeta

Córdoba

Córdoba is one of Andalucía's richest jewels. In addition to the Mezquita or Great Mosque (▶ 22), the city's old quarter of narrow streets with flower-filled balconies and patios allows visitors an insight into the essence of southern Spain. The town lies along the banks of the River Guadalquivir, overlooked by the Sierra de Córdoba. With extremes of heat in the summer and harsh winters, a good time to visit is spring or autumn.

An excellent way of exploring Córdoba is by horse and carriage

Tools found on the banks of the River Guadalquivir suggest that palaeolithic man lived here. Cordoba later became a leading centre of the people of Tartessos and was then conquered by the Carthaginians, the Romans (when it became the capital of Baetica) and the Moors.

In 929, under Moorish rule, the Caliphate of Córdoba was established. With the founding of a university, Córdoba became a renowned centre of art, culture and learning. This period saw the construction of Córdoba's great Mezquita and other fine examples of Moorish architecture.

Gradually, in the 11th and 12th centuries, Córdoba went into decline. With the breaking up of the Caliphate into small *tarifas* (states), Córdoba came under the jurisdiction of Sevilla. After it fell to the Christians in 1236, the Catholic Monarchs presided here while planning the reconquest of Granada and it was here that Queen Isabella granted Columbus the commission for his voyage of discovery.

The city has many attractions and should be explored on foot. Bear in mind that some of its narrow streets do not easily accommodate pedestrians and cars simultaneously! The Judería (old Jewish Quarter) is a delightful area of tiny streets and white houses. Brilliantly-coloured flowers adorn small squares and patios can be seen through doorways.

✚ 42C3
✉ 187km north of Málaga
🍴 Choice of restaurants (£–£££)
🚌 Estación de Autobuses, Plaza de las Tres Culturas
☎ 957 40 40 40
🚃 Estación de RENFE, Avenida de América
☎ 957 40 02 02
♿ Few
❓ Easter ceremonies; Flamenco (5–18 May); International Festival of Music, Theatre and Dance (Aug); National Festival of Folklore (Sep)
ℹ️ Tourist information: Calle Torrijos 10
12 35;
www.turisc

What to See in Córdoba

ALCÁZAR DE LOS REYES CRISTIANOS ✪

This Mudéjar-style palace was begun by King Alfonso XI in the early 14th century. Outstanding Roman mosaics, the old Moorish courtyard and baths still remain. This was once the residence of the Catholic Kings, and a one-time Moorish prison.

LA MEZQUITA (► 22, TOP TEN)

MUSEO ARQUEOLÓGICO PROVINCIAL ✪

Housed in the attractive 16th-century Palacio de los Páez, the museum has a fine collection of objects, ranging from prehistoric to Roman and Moorish times.

MUSEO DE BELLAS ARTES ✪

This fine arts museum contains paintings and sculptures by some of Spain's great masters including Goya, Luis Maroles and Alonso.

✉ Plaza Campo Santo de los Mártires
☎ 957 42 01 51
🕐 Tue–Sat 10–2, 4:30–6:30; Sun 9:30–2:30
🍴 Inexpensive (free Fri)
♿ Few

✉ Plaza Jerónimo Páez 7
☎ 957 47 40 11
🕐 Wed–Sat 9–8:30, Tue 2:30–8:30, Sun 9–2:30
♿ Few 🍴 Cheap (EU citizens free)

✉ Plaza de Potro, 1
☎ 957 47 33 45
🕐 Wed–Sat 9–8:30, Tue 2:30–8,:30 Sun 9–2:30
♿ Few 🍴 Inexpensive

MUSEO MUNICIPAL TAURINO ✪

The Municipal Bullfighting Museum, which is housed in an elegant 16th-century mansion, has an unusual and fascinating display of items and memorabilia relating to some of Córdoba's most famous bullfighters, including the legendary Manolete.

✉ Plaza Maimónides 5
☎ 957 20 10 56
🕐 Oct–Apr, Tue–Sat 10–2, 4:30–6:30, May–Sep 10–2, 6–8; Sun 9:30–2:30
🍴 Inexpensive (free Fri)
♿ Few

PALACIO DE VIANA ✪✪

The Viana Palace warrants a visit, if only to see the beautiful patios and gardens of this fine 15th-century building. There are collections of paintings, porcelain, furniture and tapestries worth seeing. Note the spendid Mudéjar ceiling above the stairway to the first floor. Visitors are given a one-hour guided tour.

✉ Rejas de Don Gome 2
☎ 957 48 01 34
🕐 Oct–May, Mon–Fri 10–1, 4–6, Sat 10–1; mid-Jun to Sep 9–2. Closed 1–15 Jun, Sun, pub hol
🍴 Inexpensive
♿ Few

TORRE DE LA CALAHORRA ✪

Housed in the 14th-century Moorish fortress across the river, the Museo Histórico (Córdoba City Museum) makes clever use of multi-vision presentations to trace the history of Córdoba at the height of its golden era.

✉ Puente Romano
☎ 957 29 39 29
🕐 Daily 10–6
🍴 Inexpensive
♿ None

Left. *Córdoba was once a great cultural centre of Europe*

Below: *the gardens of the Alcázar exude an air of tranquillity*

53

In the Know

If you only have a short time to visit the Costa del Sol, or would like to get a real flavour of the region, here are some ideas:

Ways To Be A Local

Try to speak some Spanish – even a few basic words and sentences show willing and are usually appreciated.

Shake hands when introduced – it is also normal as a form of greeting or saying goodbye.

Avoid making disparaging remarks or sarcastic jokes – the Spaniards are a proud race.

Try not to be too critical about Spain – leave that to the Spaniards, if they so wish!

Sample local dishes and do not complain if the food is different to back home.

Behave as the locals do with manners and dignity.

Show moderation with drink, like the Spaniards.

Show respect when visiting churches or cathedrals and dress with dignity, particularly in rural areas.

Dress appropriately, according to whether you are on the beach, or sightseeing. Although the customs of covering up have been relaxed, a measure of modesty should be observed.

Adapt to the Andalucian routine of eating later and venture out in the evening when the temperature has cooled down.

Good Places to Have Lunch

La Meridiana (£££)
✉ Camino de la Cruz, Marbella
☎ 952 77 61 90
🕓 Wed–Sun
Top reputation for food and service.

Restaurant Plaza (££)
✉ Espada y Urbaneja, Marbella (Casco Antiguo)
☎ 952 86 36 31
Delightful for sitting out. Specialities are *paella* and fish baked in salt.

Frutos (££)
✉ Avenida Riviera, 80, Los Alamos Torremolinos
☎ 952 38 14 50
Known for its top quality Castilian cuisine. Specialities include *jamón Ibérico*, suckling pig, leg of lamb.

Mesón El Coto (££)
✉ Ctra San Pedro to Ronda, 7km from San Pedro
☎ 952 78 66 88
Attractive setting in the mountains. Charcoal grilled baby lamb, suckling pig and rabbit specialities.

Casa Pedro (££)
✉ Quitapeñas 57, Playa el Palo, Málaga
☎ 952 99 00 13.
One of the area's earliest restaurants. Seafood prepared Malaguenian style.

La Langosta (££)
✉ Calle Bulto 53, La Carihuela, Torremolinos
☎ 952 38 43 81.
Quality restaurant of long standing, known for seafood and international dishes.

Santiago (££)
✉ Paseo Marítimo
☎ 952 77 00 78
Considered to be one of Marbella's top restaurants for fish and seafood. Pleasant position on the seafront.

Restaurante Antonio (££)
✉ Calle Muelle Rivera, Puerto Banús
☎ 952 81 35 36
One of the best restaurants overlooking the port. Speciality is sea bass baked in salt.

El Andaluz (£££)
✉ Hotel Byblos, Urb. Mijas-Golf
☎ 952 46 02 50
Excellent restaurant in attractive surroundings of Byblos Hotel. Top quality cuisine, in addition to a special buffet available at lunchtime.

Casa Luque (££)
✉ Plaza Cavana 2, Nerja
☎ 952 52 10 04
Housed in a delightful old Andalucían house. Cuisine from the north of Spain.

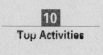

10
Top Activities

Swimming: whether in hotel pools or the sea. Look out for the EU blue flag beaches.
Sailing: all amenities available from the numerous marinas.
Waterskiing: main season Mar–Nov. Facilities available between Málaga and Estepona.
Jetskiing and windsurfing: the season is from Mar–Nov. Equipment and tuition available from hotels. Top spot for windsurfing is Tarifa.
Scuba diving: good area around Nerja; limited on western section of Costa.
Golf: the oft-referred to Costa del Golf has dozens of courses open throughout the year. *The Costa Golf*, published monthly and sold at newsstands, is useful to those interested in playing.

Tennis: many clubs on and around Costa. Most top-class hotels have courts.
Horseriding: many stables up and down the coast and in the hills.
In the Air: Hot air ballooning, flying, gliding, para-gliding and hang-gliding are all popular.
Skiing: the Sierra Nevada ski station is only 100km from the coast. Facilities include good transport, ski lifts, chair lifts and a tourist complex. Season is from Dec to Apr.

10
Top Street Markets (Baratos)

Selling a variety of goods, ranging from handicrafts and clothes to fruit and vegetables, these are fun to browse around.

Monday: Marbella, by the football stadium
Tuesday: Fuengirola
✉ Avenida Jesús

Santo Rein, Recinto Ferial and Nerja
✉ Antonio Ferrandiz Chanquote
Wednesday: Estepona
✉ Avenida Juan Carlos
Thursday: San Pedro de Alcántara (Arquillo district)
Friday: Benalmádena
✉ Arroyo de Miel
Saturday: Nueva Andalucía ✉ The Bullring and Mijas-Costa, near Euromarket
✉ Urb. El Calypso
Sunday: Estepona
✉ The Port

10
Top Beaches

Bajondillo, Torremolinos
La Carihuela, Torremolinos
Santa Ana, Benalmádena
La Vibora, between Benalmádena and Fuengirola
Playa de Los Boliches, Los Boliches
Playa de Fuengirola, Fuengirola
La Cala, between Fuengirola and Marbella
Fontanilla, Marbella
La Rada, Estepona
Cala de Maro, east of Nerja

Two locals having a gossip in Estepona

<table>
<tr><td>✚</td><td>42C1</td></tr>
<tr><td>✉</td><td>82km west of Málaga</td></tr>
<tr><td>🍴</td><td>Many restaurants and bars (£–£££)</td></tr>
<tr><td>♿</td><td>Few</td></tr>
<tr><td>↔</td><td>Puerto Duquesa (13km west) (▶ 61)</td></tr>
<tr><td>❓</td><td>Fiesta de San Isidro (15 May); local festival (early Jul); Fiesta de Virgen del Carmen (16 Jul)</td></tr>
<tr><td>ℹ</td><td>Tourist information: Avenida San Lorenzo 1 ☎ 952 80 09 13/20 02; www.estepona.es</td></tr>
</table>

ESTEPONA ✪

Some 36km west of Marbella is Estepona, another of the Costa del Sol's fast developing resorts. It offers the attractions of a long beach, pleasant seafront promenade, a marina and at least three golf courses. It is also a good centre for sailing and windsurfing.

This former fishing village retains a large fleet protected by a harbour which also has moorings for some 400 yachts and pleasure craft. An enjoyable pastime is to wander down to the port early in the morning and watch the fresh catch being sold at the fish market.

The old town dates back to Roman and Moorish times. The focal point is the charming little square of the Plaza de las Flores, entered by four archways of trees. Amid trim orange trees and tropical plants, this is a good place in which to linger over a drink. The surrounding area offers a pleasant stroll through tiny streets lined with picturesque houses. Take a look at the church on Plaza de la Roloj and go down the steps to the Mercado Municipal, a covered market for fruit, vegetables and fresh fish. Above the little town are old castle ruins.

Above and right: its picturesque old town is part of Estepona's charm

56

FRIGILIANA ✪

It is well worth taking a short drive of some 6km up into the hills from Nerja to visit Frigiliana. This pretty little village, which has won awards for its looks, spreads its dazzlingly whitewashed houses out over the hills in two sections. The older part is a mass of narrow, cobbled streets winding their way up the hillside with wonderful views over fertile orchards and the coast. Here and there you may come across a donkey patiently carrying its load. Streets and balconies are decked out with colourful flowers. The town continues to attract a growing number of visitors, with more shops and restaurants springing up all over.

One of the last battles between the Christians and the Moors was fought in the area in the 16th century, resulting in victory for the Christians. The tale of this glorious event is related by way of a series of ceramic tiles on the walls of the houses.

FUENTE VAQUEROS ✪

Fuente Vaqueros is home to the **Casa Museo García Lorca**. The museum was the former home of the poet and playwright Federico García Lorca, who was born in Fuente Vaqueros in 1898. Lorca, who spent much time in nearby Granada, became known for the sensitivity of his poetry and the powerful drama of his plays, such as *Yerma*, *Blood Wedding* and *The House of Bernarda Alba*, which continue to be widely produced on stage throughout the world. He was assassinated near Víznar during the Spanish Civil War.

✚ 47E2
✉ 56km east of Málaga
🍴 Some restaurants (££)
🚌 Local
♿ Few
↔ Nerja (➤ 69)
❷ Día de la Cruz (3 May); Feria de San Antonio (13 Jun)
ℹ Tourist information: Plaza del Ingenio, s/n ☎ 952 53 31 26

Above: *handicrafts for sale in the village*
Left: *a view of Frigiliana*

✚ 47E4
✉ 17km west of Granada
Casa Museo Federico García Lorca
✉ Calle poeta García Lorca, 4
☎ 958 51 64 53
🕐 Tue–Sun 10–1, 4 8 (winter 4–6). Tours hourly
💲 Inexpensive
♿ Few

+ 46C2
✉ 29km west of Málaga
🍴 Many restaurants (£–£££)
🚌 Corner Avenida Ramón y Cajal and Calle Alfonso XIII
🚊 RENFE station at Avenida Jesús Santos Rein (half hourly service to Málaga)
♿ Good
↔ Mijas (► 23), Parque Aquático (► 107)
❓ Fiesta de la Virgen del Carmen (16 Jul) in Los Boliches; Romería (late Sep) from Fuengirola; Fería del Rosario (7 Oct)
ℹ Tourist Information: Paseo Jesús Santos Rein 6 ☎ 952 46 74 57; www.fuengirola.org

The old art of fishing still plays an important role in the modern lifestyle of today's international resorts

FUENGIROLA ★

Some 9km west of Benalmádena Costa is the prominent resort of Fuengirola. It has changed unrecognisably from its earlier days as a peaceful little fishing village. Now the scene is one of solid high-rise apartment blocks and buildings. The old part of the town, however, presents another side of Fuengirola. A lively meeting place is the Plaza de la Constitución, which is dominated by Fuengirola's main church. The old fishermen's district of Santa Fé has plenty of character and high above the town is the old Moorish Castle, Castillo de Sohail.

The Castle, which is thought to have originated with the Romans, was rebuilt by the Moors only to be destroyed in the 15th century during the Christian reconquest of the region. The present structure dates from 1730 when it was again reinforced as protection against the British. The castle is now being converted into a cultural centre. A walk up here is recommended for excellent views of the coast.

Fuengirola is much favoured by northern Europeans who come here for extended stays to escape their native winters. There are many English-run bars and souvenir shops to be found here and in neighbouring Los Boliches. The summer season is always lively; the long sweep of beach especially appeals to families. Fuengirola has several other attractions geared to children, such as the small zoo, an Aquapark at nearby Mijas Costa and the ever-popular Tivoli World up the road.

All kinds of watersports can be enjoyed here too, including sailing, waterskiing and windsurfing. The resort has an attractive yacht club and marina, along with an extended promenade, the Paseo Marítimo, which links Fuengirola, Los Boliches and Carvajal. The former fishing village of Los Boliches has become an extension of Fuengirola, its beach lined with apartment blocks, bars and restaurants. Further east is the small resort of Carvajal, which has so far retained a more Spanish flavour.

Along the Coast to Gibraltar

This drive takes you along the coast through the Sotogrande development to the tiny British colony of Gibraltar.

From Estepona take the N340 coastal road southwest in the direction of Algeciras.

The road follows the coast fairly closely for a while, passing through a string of *urbanizaciones* (developments). Some 10 minutes on you may wish to turn off and take a look at Duquesa Marina (follow the signs), another of the Costa's yacht filled harbours.

Continue on N340.

You will soon enter the province of Cádiz and the community of Manilva. The road then passes through Sotogrande (known for golf and polo). Shortly after is a turning to Puerto Sotogrande, another marina.

Continue on the N340.

This last section of the coastal road has been widened to dual carriageway. Ticket offices advertising ferry trips to Tangier and Centa signal the approach to the ferry ports.

Soon after, look for the turn-off to La Linea and follow the signs to La Linea–Gibraltar, 7km. Drive to La Linea and continue to the border with Gibraltar.

As you can encounter lengthy delays at the border when re-entering Spain, depending on the current political situation, in addition to parking problems in Gibraltar itself, you are strongly advised to leave your car in the car park in La Linea. There are ticket machines, with free parking on Sundays. Cross into Gibraltar on foot (you will need to show your passport). Guides are lined up here, ready to take you on a 60–90-minute tour, which includes a drive through town and up to St Michael's Cave where you can see dramatic rock formations. The drive continues steeply up through hairpin bends to see the apes and the sweeping views of the Mediterranean, Atlantic and south to Africa.

Return to La Linea and take the N240 back to Estepona.

The Rock of Gibraltar is an impressive landmark which can be seen for miles along the coast

Distance
105km

Time
About 6 hours, allowing time to visit Gibraltar

Start/end point
Estepona
✚ 42C1

Lunch
Da Paolo (££)
✉ The Tower, Admiral's Walk, Gibraltar
☎ 9567 76 799

+ 46A2
⊠ 120km west of Málaga
🍴 Several restaurants
🚌 Local bus services
♿ Few
↔ Casares (► 18)
? Romería San Juan (23
  Jun); Fería Virgen de las
  Nieves (second week
  Aug); Fiesta de Santo
  Niño (8, 9 and 10 Sep)
ℹ Tourist information: Calle
  Fuente 91, Casares
  ☎ 952 89 41 26

GAUCÍN ★

Situated about 40 minutes away from the coast between
Casares and Ronda, Gaucín is yet another of those
enchanting little white towns you will come across
travelling around the Andalucían countryside. As you
approach you will be confronted by a cluster of whitewashed houses, topped by red roofs, spread out beneath a
cluster of cracked rocks.

The old Moorish fortress, Castillo de Aguila (Eagle's
Castle), now partly restored, stands high above the village,
forming a silhouette against the backdrop of mountains.
From this vantage point there are magnificent views
across the valley of the Guadiaro river, reaching out to the
coastline as far as the Rock of Gibraltar.

*The little white town of
Gaucín nestles below a
great rock massif
crowned by an old
Moorish castle*

The village is delightful and abounds with colourful
flowers and plants. Its narrow streets and one-way system
are not conducive to driving, however, and the place is
best explored on foot. The daily fish market is always a
lively event.

Gaucín makes a good base from which to explore the
hinterland, which is dotted about with attractive towns and
villages such as Ronda, Grazalema, Casares, Ubrique and
Jimena de la Frontera.

Granada

Granada is the capital of its province, the see of an archbishop and a university town. In addition to La Alhambra, with which Granada is so closely associated, the city has much else to commend it: its beautiful setting, built on three hills backed by the snowy peaks of the Sierra Nevada, its historic links with the past and significant religious festivals. A visit to

Granada could be made from the coast within a day. However, more time is recommended to explore one of Spain's crowning glories, the last kingdom of the Moors.

Known as Iliberis during the Iberian culture, Granada was taken by the Romans and the Visigoths before its conquest by the Moors in 711. The 11th century saw the decline of the Caliphate of Córdoba and the beginning of the Kingdom of Granada. From the 13th century, until its downfall at the end of the 15th century, Granada flourished as a prosperous cultural centre with the construction of magnificent buildings such as La Alhambra (➤ 17). In 1492 Granada was taken by the Catholic Monarchs. This marked the end of Moorish rule and Spain's history was changed. Granada continued to prosper during the Renaissance but a decline set in after the repression of a Moorish uprising in the 16th century.

The priority for most visitors is the palace of La Alhambra. Magical as this Moorish palace is, it is surrounded by some equally fascinating places. The summer palace of El Generalife, with its shady avenues, water gardens, fountains and airy gazebos, is a neighbour of La Alhambra that you really should visit. On the slopes of the hill facing La Alhambra is the picturesque old Moorish quarter of Albaicín, a labyrinth of steep, narrow streets and small squares which has changed little with time. To the east rises the hill of Sacramonte, formerly the home of cave-dwelling gypsies.

47F4

129km northeast of Málaga

Variety of bars and restaurants (£–£££)

Estación de Autobuses, Carretera de Jaén s/n
958 18 54 80/98

Estación de FFCC, Avenida de Andalucía s/n
958 20 40 00

Few

Día de la Toma (1, 2 Jan); Semana Santa (Easter); Corpus Christi; International Music and Dance Festival (end Jun, early Jul); Romería (29 Sep); International jazz Festival (Nov)

Tourist information: Corral del Carbón, Plaza de Mariana Pineda, 10 Bajo 958 24 /1 28; www.turismodegranada.es

Close by La Alhambra are the peaceful gardens of the Generalife, former summer palace of Moorish kings

Inside the Capilla Real

Oficios 3 (Cathedral)

958 22 78 48

1 Apr–31 Oct Mon–Sat 10:30–1, 4–7, Sun 11–1, 4–7

Inexpensive

RENFE station Granada

Few

Antequerela Alta 11

958 22 21 89

Oct–Mar Tue–Fri 10–1, 4–7, Sat and Sun 10–1

Inexpensive

Few

What to See in Granada

CAPILLA REAL ✪✪

The Royal Chapel, sanctioned by the Catholic Monarchs for their burial, was begun in 1506 and completed under the reign of Hapsburg Emperor Charles V in 1521. It has a richly adorned interior. In the chancel, closed by a screen, are the mausoleums of King Ferdinand and Queen Isabella, along with their daughter Juana la Loca and her husband Philip the Fair. A museum reached through the north arm of the transept displays items of historical interest and a fine collection of paintings and sculpture.

CASA MANUEL DE FALLA ✪

Manuel de Falla (1876–1946) was born in Cadiz and taught by Pedrell, the founder of Spain's modern national school of composition. He spent several years in Paris, but drew on his own native musical traditions in works such as the popular ballet music *The Three-Cornered Hat*. The composer lived in this house for a number of years. Items on display relate to his life.

Did you know ?

In January 1492 the Boy King, Boabdil, last Moorish ruler, finally surrendered Granada to the Catholic Monarchs. Looking back on Granada as he went away into exile he is said to have wept, only to be rebuked by his mother with words to the effect that: 'You weep like a woman for what you could not hold as a man.' The spot has ever since been known as the Suspiro del Moro *(the Moor's Sigh). It is a few kilometres east of Granada on the road to Motril.*

The Boy King Boabdil surrenders the keys of Granada to the Catholics

CATEDRAL ✪

The cathedral was begun in 1528 on the orders of the Catholic Monarchs. Construction was under the great master Diego de Siloé, and continued after his death in 1528. It features a magnificent Capilla Real (Royal Chapel) and has a notable rotunda, with some fine paintings by Alonso Cano, a native of Granada.

✉ Gran Via b
☎ 958 22 29 59
⏱ Mon–Sat 10:30–1:30, 4–7, Sun 4–7
✋ Inexpensive ♿ Few

MONASTERIO DE LA CARTUJA ✪

This former Carthusian Monastery, which dates back to the 16th century, has a worthwhile collection of paintings and sculpture.

✉ Paseo de la Cartuja, s/n
☎ 958 16 19 32
⏱ Mon–Sat 10–1, 4–6:30
✋ Inexpensive (free Sun)

MUSEO ARQUEOLÓGICO ✪

The museum is housed in the Casa Castril, an elegant Renaissance palace, noted for its delicately carved plateresque doorway. It has a fine collection of ceramics from Roman and Moorish times, in addition to some superb Egyptian vases unearthed in the region.

✉ Carrera del Darro 41
☎ 958 22 56 40
⏱ Wed–Sat 9–6, Tue 2:30–6, Sun 9–2:30
✋ Inexpensive (EU citizens free) ♿ Few

➕ 46B2

✉ 56km west of Málaga

🍴 Wide range of restaurants, many (£££)

🚌 Bus station, Avenida del Trapiche, s/n ☎ 952 76 44 00. Avenida Ricardo Soriano for local services

♿ Few

❓ Carnival (pre-Lent), Fería de la Virgen del Carmen (16 Jul), Fería de San Bernabé Patrón (Jun), Fería de San Pedro (Oct)

ℹ Glorieta de la Fontanilla, Paseo Marítimo ☎ 952 77 14 42. Plaza de los Naranjos ☎ 952 82 35 50

Arco de Marbello

✉ CN-340, Km 183.5

☎ 952 82 28 18

Bonsai Museum

✉ Parque Arroyo de la Represa

☎ 952 86 29 26

🕐 Daily 10–1:30, 4:30–8

🚌 Avenida Ricardo Soriano

👣 Inexpensive ♿ Few

Above right: *the seafront*
Below: *motorists pass under the arch*

MARBELLA ●●

Marbella is synonymous with the concept of a hedonistic world for the jet set. Since its meteoric rise to fame, Marbella has indeed never ceased to set itself above its fellow resorts along the coast, by continuing to cultivate its image as a playground of the rich and famous with their luxury yachts and glamorous life-styles.

Marbella's development can be traced back to the 1940s, with the founding of the El Rodeo restaurant and inn by the Spanish aristocrat Ricardo Soriano. His nephew, Prince Alfonso Hohenlohe of Liechtenstein, went on to develop a small beach property into the Marbella Club chalet complex for his friends among the international set. This continued to attract celebrities to the area and led to the construction of a string of luxurious hotels which were built along the coast on either side of Marbella town, offering beautiful gardens, pools and sports facilities.

After the halcyon days of the '70s and early '80s, there was an economic slump. Marbella went into a decline and began to wane in popularity. Then in the early 1990s, ambitious programmes were put forward to give the resort a much needed facelift. The remodelling of the Paseo Marítimo, the planting of palms and beautifying of the beaches, along with the construction of sorely needed underground car parks and pledges to clean the place up in general, did much to restore Marbella's image and prestige. Marbella continues to prosper and grow. Urban developments spread out in all directions, while more projects are underway to propagate the image of the 'New Marbella'.

There are several Marbellas – the town itself, now a busy commercial centre, the beachfront and marina, and its picturesque old quarter, the Casco Antiguo (Old Town) (► 21). In the centre of Marbella town there are plush apartments overlooking the sea. From the Casco Antiguo a short walk will take you to the Parque de la Alameda (Alameda Park). The pleasant little park features exotic plants, trees and fountains, with attractively tiled benches adding to the scene. Stroll down to the beachfront through the Avenida del Mar, a broad pedestrianised avenue adorned with flowers and trees and a series of lively Salvador Dalí sculptures.

The Paseo Marítimo, which stretches far on either side of town, offers an enjoyable seafront stroll, with bars and restaurants lining the route. Many improvements which have been made to the long stretch of beach, shaded at regular intervals by palm trees. Have a wander around the Puerto Deportivo (yacht harbour), where you can linger over a drink or a meal.

Two museums (in and around the Old Town) are worth a visit; the **Museo Bonsai**, for its delightful collection of Japanese-style miniature trees and the **Museo del Grabado Español Contemporáneo** (Museum of Spanish Contemporary Prints) for its exhibitions which include works by prominent Spanish artists.

Museum of Spanish Contemporary Prints

✉ Hospital Bazán s/n
🕐 Mon–Fri 10–2, 5:30–8:30, Sun 10–2
🚌 Avenida Ricardo Soriano
♿ Few

All kinds of styles make up the face of modern Marbella

Above: *taking a ride in a horse and buggy is always a pleasantly relaxing way of enjoying your surroundings*
Right: *an old and impressive disused aqueduct outside Nerja*

The municipality of Marbella covers a 28km stretch of coastline, which stretches from the marina and the residential area of Cabo Pino, east of the town, to Guadalmina out to the west. The section from Marbella to Guadalmina has come to be known as the Golden Mile, so named for the concentration of luxurious hotels, restaurants and golf courses to be found here. Expensive villas with pools, set amidst gardens of lush, tropical vegetation complete the picture.

References to the 'exclusive resort of Marbella' can be misleading as, more often than not, the term applies not to the town, but to the hotels strung out on either side of the town, including the plush Guadalmina development and the Puerto Banús marina. This area is, in effect, the 'playground' of the jet set.

Puerto Banús (► 24–5) is officially part of San Pedro de Alcántara (► 78, located 3km away) and is usually listed under Nueva Andalucía. However, it is within the community of Marbella and tends to be included in references to the town. It continues to be a place of pure enjoyment and a magnet for yachties. The marina has berths for over 900 and attracts craft of all sizes; millionaires' yachts are a common sight. There are also facilities for many watersports.

Marbella continues to attract the celebrities and stars. The partying goes on but has become less visible as more of the social scene takes place privately. This does not deter many visitors, however, who may well catch sight of some familiar face.

Did you know ?

The most luxurious properties are to be seen in the surroundings of Marbella, particularly in the areas of Nueva Andalucía and Guadalmina. Amidst all this opulence is a palace belonging to King Fahd of Saudi Arabia. Referred to as the White House for its resemblance, in miniature, to its namesake in Washington, it stands out as a landmark in the hills, with a grand mosque, alongside, to keep it company.

MIJAS (► 23, TOP TEN)

NERJA ✪✪✪

Nerja lies in a fertile valley of fruit orchards, known mainly for the production of peaches and pomegranates. Its attractive setting amidst cliffs overlooking rocky coves below have earned its reputation as the jewel of the eastern Costa del Sol. Its name is derived from the old Moorish word *naricha*, meaning 'rich in water'. The town started life as a Moorish farming estate during the 10th

☗ 47E2
✉ 52km east of Málaga
🍴 Wide choice of restaurants and bars (£–£££)
🚌 Bus connections
♿ Few
🔁 Maro (4km east)

Above and right: *Nerja's picturesque coastal setting is its greatest attraction*

? Carnival (pre-Lent); Semana Santa (Easter); Cruces de Mayo (3 May); Fiesta de la Virgen del Carmen (16 Jul); Feriá de Nerja (13 Oct)

i Tourist information: Puerta del Mar 4 ☎ 952 52 15 31

century, a centre of the silk and sugar industries for the area. All reminders of its Moorish past and much of the town were destroyed in the earthquake of 1884.

Nerja stands out as the most appealing of the resorts east of Málaga. It retains the charm of its old town with its narrow streets, many pedestrianised, and lined with whitewashed houses that are adorned with flowers, and crammed with restaurants. These streets lead down to Nerja's best-known feature and focal point, the Bálcon de Europa. This curved promontory, lined with palm trees overlooking the bay is a favoured spot for keen photographers. A series of steps will take you down to the Paseo de los Caribineros and a walkway onto the popular Plays de Burriana.

Although Nerja has grown into an internationally popular resort over the years, it has so far managed to escape the sort of development found along much of its neighbouring western coastline. Most noticeably Nerja has managed to retain its small-town atmosphere. Now linked to Málaga by the Autovía del Mediterraneo, expansion is inevitably on its way, with some new developments to be seen along the seafront.

Some 4km east of Nerja lies the little village of Maro. Perched on a clifftop above a small cove, the village offers good views of the coastline. Of interest is the attractive little church of Nuestra Señora de las Maravillas de Maro, and the 4-tiered aqueduct.

Did you know ?

Nerja's famous promenade received its name when King Alfonso XII was touring the area to show sympathy following an earthquake which hit the town on Christmas Day in 1884. While visiting Nerja he stood on the promontory, with its magnificent view of the Mediterranean, and then and there declared it the Balcón de Europa *(Balcony of Europe). The name stuck.*

Food & Drink

Much of the best natural produce of the Costa del Sol provides the basis for the region's cuisine. Fresh fish, such as sardines, squid, octopus, hake, crayfish and cod are plentiful and widely available. Fruit is produced locally in the fertile orchards to be found to the east of Málaga. Some of the more exotic include peaches, pomegranates, grapes and melons. Olive oil refined in Málaga and olives themselves are of high quality and the cured hams of Trévelez are unequalled.

Local Specialities

As with other tourist destinations, many restaurants on the Costa del Sol provide international cuisine to suit all tastes. But try to search out a menu that includes some typical dishes from the region. You are most likely to find good traditional cooking in smaller eateries inland, away from popular tourist spots.

Fresh grilled fish eaten al fresco

Cold soups are popular starters. Featuring prominently is *gaspacho andaluz*, a tomato based chilled soup, usually served with side dishes. Lesser known, but also delicious, are *salmorejo*, a variant and thicker version of *gaspacho* and *ajo blanco*, based on crushed garlic and almonds, often served with grapes. *Sopa de rape* is among the many excellent fish soups you can find.

Fritura malagueña is typical of coastal cooking, an assortment of fried fish. Other dishes to look out for are cod *à la Málaga*, fish chowders, casserole of dogfish, cockles, crayfish and prawns grilled or served *al pil-pil* (sizzling with garlic). Roasted sardines and fresh anchovies can

Did you know ?

Chiringuitos *is the name given to beach bars and restaurants. They are to be found all along the coast, ranging from simple open air huts, where the emphasis is casual, to more sophisticated eateries. These are often very good places to sample good traditional Spanish dishes, with an emphasis on fresh fish and seafood, either fried or grilled and served with a simple salad.*

also be delicious and rice dishes such as a *risotto à la marinera* (seafood) or *paella* are usually a good bet.

Habas à la rondeña (broad beans Ronda-style), *pimientos à la malaguena* (peppers Málaga-style) are other local dishes to sample. *Puchero* is a sort of country casserole with chickpeas.

Up in the hills above Málaga you can come across tasty varieties of sausages from the different regions. Try the *morcillas* of Antequera, *embutidos* from Ronda and *chorizo* produced in Benaofán. *Conejo* (rabbit) or *pollo al ajillo* (chicken with garlic) are popular dishes and kid is also a delicacy here. The Alpujarras is famous for its hams and produces succulent pork dishes, such as suckling pig.

Worth a mention among the desserts are *yemas del tajo*, based on egg yolks and sugar, *dulce de membrillo*, made from quinces and there is always the ubiquitous *flan* (crème caramel). A very typical way to round off a meal, however, is with the fresh fruit of the season.

Above: *take-away stalls for fruit and drinks are plentiful*
Below: *Mijas has its share of food stalls*

Wine

Málaga is known for its wines. Although there are dry varieties it is famous primarily for its sweet wines, produced from the grapes of Antequera, La Axarquía.

Some excellent sweet dessert wines are also grown in the vineyards around Competa where it is possible to try wine-tasting. Further inland, some very acceptable wines are produced in the Montilla-Moriles area. Although not a local product, a jug of *sangría* (red wine, fruit and lemonade), served chilled with ice, is a pleasant accompaniment to a meal on a warm day. A popular liqueur is *aguardiente de Ojén*.

RINCÓN DE LA VICTORIA ✪

Lying some 12km east of Málaga, Rincón de la Victoria is a fast developing resort. It offers a pleasant new seafront promenade, some modest accommodation, an 18-hole golf course, riding, tennis and boats for hire. The resort has a reputation for good fish restaurants, a speciality being a small sardine-type fish known as *victorianos* and *coquinas* (clams). The Wednesday market is always a great event.

RONDA ✪✪✪

Ronda is renowned for its spectacular setting. The views of the ravine and surrounding landscapes, its historical background and legends of bandits, all add to a certain mystique, which continues to attract visitors. A mighty split in the El Tajo gorge, spanned by the Puente Nuevo (▶ 26), divides the town into Old Ronda (La Ciudad) and the newer part, known as El Mercadillo.

Most monuments of note are in the old town, which retains Moorish influences. These include the imposing church of Santa Maria la Mayor, the Minaret of San Sebastian, the Palacio de Mondragón and the Casa del Gigante, the Palacio del Marqués de Salvatierra and the gardens of the Casa del Rey Moro. The Museo Lara (Science and History) and Museo del Bandolero (History and Legends of local bandits) are also worth a visit. The café-lined Plaza del Socorro is the focal point of the newer part of town, Ronda's main shopping centre, with more magnificent views to be seen from the attractive gardens of the Alameda del Tajo, near by.

Ronda has long-standing associations with bullfighting. The bullring, near the Puente Nuevo, was built in 1785 and is the oldest in Spain. It was here that the rules of modern bullfighting were laid down by Francisco Romero, whose

Above: *shrine of the Virgen del Carmen in Rincón de la Victoria*
Right: *Ronda's bullring is one of the oldest in Spain*

grandson Pedro Romero went on to become one of Spain's most famous matadors. The bullring, now owned by Antonio Ordoñez, another of the greats, is used only for special fiestas. The bullfighting museum behind the ring contains glittering costumes, gear and a wealth of photographs relating to the world of bullfighting.

Ronda is a city with a romantic past. Two famous Americans, writer Ernest Hemingway and actor Orson Welles, were keen followers of the bullfight. Both spent much time here and each of them formed a close friendship with Ordoñez. By his request, Orson Welles' ashes are scattered over the bulfighter's nearby ranch.

Some 20km southwest of Ronda is the **Cueva de la Pileta** (Pileta Cave), which has significant prehistoric rock paintings of animals, outlined in black and red, believed to date back to over 25,000 years ago. The illustrated figures include bison, deer, horses and a large fish.

Cueva de la Pileta

➕ 46A2

✉ 20km southwest of Ronda

☎ 952 16 73 43

🕐 Daily 10–1, 4–6; tours last about one hour

✋ Inexpensive   ♿ Few

Did you know ?

The Austrian romantic poet Rainer María Rilke, who came here in 1913 to recuperate from an illness, wrote of Ronda: 'Everywhere I sought the dreamt of city and at last I have found it.' His room at the Reina Victoria Hotel has been kept much as it was and preserved as a tiny museum. A key may be requested at reception to visit the room, which contains some photographs and verses written by Rilke during his stay. His sensitivity is well portrayed in the statue which stands in the garden.

In & Around
Ronda

Distance
4km

Time
2–3 hours

Start/end point
Plaza de España
➕ 46A2

Lunch
Pedro Romero (££)
✉ Virgen de la Paz 18, Ronda
☎ 952 87 11 10

This walk starts in the Plaza de España and takes you across the bridge to explore the old town of Ronda.

From the Plaza de España walk towards the Puente Nuevo (New Bridge).

Take a walk around the Parador, on your right, for spectacular views of the gorge.

Return and cross over the bridge.

Look down into the ravine as you pass. A right turn down Calle Tenorio will take you into a network of narrow streets and neat white houses to the Plaza del Campillo.

Keep walking and at the far end look for steps leading down the hill.

A short walk down reveals Ronda's houses perched on the clifftop. A further walk down will provide you with the classic view of the bridge, but it's a long climb up!

Back up again take the small street ahead to the Plaza Mondragón.

On the right is the Palacio de Mondragón, once a Moorish palace.

Continue to Plaza de la Duquesa de Parcént. A left turn leads to the entrance of the Colegiata de Santa María la Mayor. Take the short slope down to Calle Armiñian and turn left. Note the Minaret of San Sebastian before crossing over to turn sharp right.

There are fine carvings on the façade of the Palacio del Marqués de Salvatierra (closed to the public).

Climb up Calle Santo Domingo to the Casa del Rey Moro, where you can take a long winding staircase down to the river and back up again to the gardens. Rejoin Calle Armiñán and cross back over the bridge to the Plaza de España.

Below the town are plenty of walking areas from which to appreciate Ronda's spectacular setting above

The small white town of Salobreña reaches up the hillside to the old Moorish castle known as El Capricho.

SALOBREÑA

Some 13km east of Almuñecar is the attractive little town of Salobreña, now within the stretch of coast known as the Costa Tropical. It lies a short distance from the sea among fruit orchards and sugarcane plantations.

Salobreña features a cluster of whitewashed houses sprawling up the hill, dominated by the old Moorish *alcázar* known as El Capricho. The castle has been well restored and offers magnificent views of the coast, surrounding countryside and the beautiful peaks of the Sierra Nevada. Also worth a visit is the 16th-century church of Nuestra Señora del Rosario, which was built on the site of an old mosque.

Much of Salobreña's charm lies in the fact that it remains relatively unspoilt, with few hotels and restaurants. It provides a good gateway to Granada, however, and can receive quite an influx of visitors, especially at weekends. From here it is only 4km further along the coast to Motril, principally known as a commercial centre for sugarcane and chemicals. Take a look at the Sanctuary of Our Lady of the Head, which stands atop the hill. Enthusiasts enjoy the golf course, located between the two.

47F2

93 km east of Málaga

Choice of restaurants (£–£££)

Bus connections

Few

Almuñecar (13km west, ➤ 42)

Semana Santa (Easter); Fiesta de San Juan y San Pedro (end Jul); Fiesta do Nuestra Señora del Rosario (early Oct)

Tourist information: Plaza de Goya s/n ☎ 958 61 03 14

A quiet spot in the heart of San Pedro de Alcántara, a town which has been nicely rejuvenated

🗺 46B1
✉ 70km west of Málaga
🍴 Choice of restaurants and bars (£–£££)
🚻 Few
ℹ Tourist information: Avenida Marques del Duero, 69 ☎ 952 78 52 52

Alco de San Pedro
✉ CN 340, Km 170.5
☎ 925 78 13 60

SAN PEDRO DE ALCÁNTARA ✪

San Pedro Alcántara has undergone a facelift in recent years, with pleasing results. A development programme incorporating a new coastal promenade and beach improvements, stretching from Puerto Banús to Guadalmina, has given it a boost as an increasingly popular resort.

On the northern side of the coastal road is the small town itself, which has a neat, pleasant appearance. The Calle Marqués del Duero, attractively shaded by orange trees and palms, and lined with shops and cafés, leads up the hill to the small square of Plaza de la Iglesia adorned by a fountain. Adjacent to the town hall is San Pedro's parish church. Its white façade framed by two palm trees makes an attractive picture.

San Pedro is the first centre in Spain to have introduced the sport of cable skiing, which involves the water skier being towed by cable for long distances.

Three archaeological sites in the vicinity are worth exploring: the 6th-century Visigoth Basílica de Vega del Mar, the Villa Romana de Río Verde, remnants of a Roman villa from the 1st century, and Las Bovedas where the remains of old Roman thermal baths can be seen.

🗺 42C1
✉ 100km west of Málaga
🍴 Wide choice
🚌 Bus connections
🚻 Few
🎪 San Roque Annual Fair (early Sep); Sotogrande golf tournaments, polo matches (Jul, Aug, Sep)
ℹ Avda 20 Abril s/n, La Línea ☎ 956 76 99 50

SAN ROQUE/SOTOGRANDE ✪

This is *the* place for big time golfers and is said to feature Spain's highest proportion of registered golfers in any one centre. Among the four golf courses, the Valderrama Robert Trent Jones Course played host to the 1997 Ryder Cup. Polo is also played here during the summer and the Sotogrande Marina is another attraction.

The little town is an attractive centre in itself with narrow streets and plenty of flowers and plants. The lively cafés and restaurants of the Campamento area appeal to a younger crowd.

A Tour of Andalucían Towns & Villages

This drive takes you into the rugged landscape of the Serranía de Ronda and through several of the region's most attractive mountain towns.

From the east side of San Pedro de Alcántara, take the turning to Ronda (➤ 74).

The A376, (Ruta de la Serranía de Ronda) is fairly wide and has a good surface as it twists its way up into the mountains offering fine views. The route takes you through pine forests, rocks and white cliffs, until Ronda comes into view, about an hour later (50km). Allow time to visit Ronda and have some lunch at the restaurant which offers a dramatic view of the steep cliff on which the town is built.

Return through the old town and take the A369, in the direction of Algeciras, to Gaucín(➤ 62).

This section passes through barren hills and rocks and wide open vistas and includes a bad stretch of road. Take a look at the delightful white hillside town of Gaucín.

Join the A377, direction Manilva-Algeciras. Some 16km on take a sharp left turn to the photogenic town of Casares (➤ 18).

This road leads shortly to a stunning view of this white Andalucían town sprawled over the hillside. Continue towards the town and take a left fork uphill for an even more spectacular sight of the town, crowned by the old fortress.

Follow the signs to Estepona and take the old road, which winds its way down through fertile country to the coast. You should reach Estepona some 25 minutes later (➤ 56). Rejoin N340 and head east back to San Pedro.

Distance
145km

Time
About 8 hours

Start/end point
San Pedro de Alcántara
✚ 46B1

Lunch
Hotel-Restaurante Don Miguel, Ronda (££)
✉ Villanueva 4 y 8, Ronda
☎ 952 87 10 90

As a contrast to the golfing world of neighbouring Sotogrande, San Roque has a few attractions of its own

Sevilla

Sevilla is the capital of Andalucía and Spain's fourth largest city. It is dominated by La Giralda and the great cathedral that this minaret tower adjoins (➤ 20). Various cultures have left their mark here, from the Romans to the Moors and the Christians. An early carving on the Jerez Gate alludes to the legendary origins of the city: 'Hercules built me, Caesar surrounded me with walls and towers, the King Saint took me.'

Sevilla is believed to have been founded by the Iberians. Subsequent occupiers included the Greeks, Phoenicians and the Carthaginians (who named it Hispalis). Around 205 BC the town was taken over by the Romans and it continued to flourish under Julius Caesar. During the 5th century AD it became the capital of the Visigoths. It was captured in 712 by the Moors, whose long occupation has left magnificent traces of their artistic merits.

In 1248 Sevilla was reconquered by Ferdinand III of Castile. But it was the discovery of America which brought fame and prosperity to Sevilla, when Christopher Columbus returned here from his first voyage in 1493. In the 16th and 17th centuries the port became the most important in Spain. During this period, often described as Spain's Golden Age, the Sevilla school of painters brought great prestige to the city.

Sevilla is a city to explore on foot with the cathedral a good focal point from which to start. The medieval quarter of the Barrio Santa Cruz, near by, is a delightful maze of narrow streets and whitewashed houses adorned with wrought iron balconies, decked with flowers.

A stroll around town reveals mansions, squares and lovely parks, such as the Parque de Maria Luisa, the Murillo gardens and those of the Reales Alcazares. The large Plaza de España contains a tiny canal, decorated bridges and fountains. An imposing crescent is adorned with ceramic tiles depicting Spain's provincial capitals.

Over the bridge is the Triana area, home of the gypsy population. Alternative ways of getting around are by 'SevillaTour' buses or with style in a horse-drawn carriage.

Well known as the setting for *Carmen* and other famous operas, Sevilla has long had a romantic image. In the spring, when the heady scent of orange blossom gives Sevilla a special atmosphere, the unique celebrations of Semana Santa (Holy Week) and the exuberant Feria de Sevilla take place (➤ 116).

✚ 42B2

✉ 219km northwest of Málaga

🍴 Huge choice of restaurants and *tapas* bars for which the city is famed

🚌 Bus stations: Prado de San Sebastian ☎ 954 41 71 11 & Plaza de Armas ☎ 954 90 77 37

♿ Few

🚉 Estación de FFCC Santa Justa, Avenida Kansas City s/n ☎ 954 54 02 02

❓ Semana Santa (Easter), Feria de Sevilla (2 weeks after Easter), Corpus Christi, Fiesta de la Virgen de los Reyes (15 Aug)

ℹ Avenida de la Constitucion 21 B ☎ 954 22 14 04

Left: *horse and carriage in the Maria Luisa Park*

Isla Mágica

Theme park dedicated to the Century of the Discoveries

✉ Isla de la Cartuja

☎ 902 16 17 16

🕐 Varies, check locally

💶 Expensive

🍴 Bars and restaurant

🚌 C1, C2, SevillaTour bus

♿ Few

River Walk and Cruise

A stroll along the banks of the River Guadalquivir evokes a strong sense of Sevilla's past. A left turn from the town centre will take you past La Maestranza, one of Spain's top bullrings, the Maestranza Theatre, the Torre de Oro, converted in to a small museum, and the Palacio de San Telmo. 'Cruceros Turísticos Torre del Oro' operate one-hour boat cruises along the river (departures from the 'Torre del Oro' dock. ☎ 954 21 12 42

What to See in Sevilla

CASA DE PILATOS ✪✪✪

This 16th-century private mansion is one of Sevilla's jewels. Combining Mudéjar, Gothic and Renaissance styles, its patios, archways and salons are adorned with delicate carving, tilework and wooden coffered ceilings. A grand staircase leads to the upper floors, which contain a collection of art. The adjoining gardens may also be visited.

🖂 Plaza Pilatos 1
☎ 954 22 52 98
🕐 Daily 9–6
🚌 C1, C2, C3, C4
♿ Good
🖐 Inexpensive (free Tue PM)

MUSEO ARQUEOLÓGICO ✪✪✪

Housed in the Renaissance palace built for the 1929 Ibero-America Exhibition, the Archeological Museum has a fine collection of objects from prehistory and the Moorish culture. Outstanding among its exhibits is the Carombolo Treasure; from the 7th century this includes gold jewellery from the Tartessos civilisation.

🖂 Plaza de América
☎ 954 23 24 01
🕐 Wed–Sat 9–8, Tue 3–8, Sun, pub hol 9–2
🖐 Inexpensive (EU citizens free)
♿ Few

MUSEO DE BELLAS ARTES ✪✪✪

Housed in the former Convento de la Merced, the museum contains a splendid collection of fine art with paintings and sculpture, ceramics and weapons. Room V contains works of art by some of the great Spanish masters, including Zurbarán and Murillo.

REALES ALCÁZARES ✪✪✪

Former Moorish palaces, largely rebuilt for Christian kings after the reconquest of Sevilla: the centrepiece, Palacio Mudéjar del Rey Don Pedro, built by Pedro I in the 14th century, is a superb example of Mudéjar art. Salons, archways and columns are richly decorated with exquisite carvings, ceramics and wooden ceilings. Note the dome ceiling of the Salón de Embajadores (Hall of Ambassadors).

⊠ Plaza Museo 9
☎ 954 22 07 90
🕐 Wed–Sat 9–8, Tue 3–8, Sun, pub hol 9–2
🎟 Inexpensive (EU citizens free)
♿ Few

⊠ Plaza del Triunfo
☎ 954 50 23 23
🕐 Tue–Sat 9:30–7, Sun 9:30–5
🎟 Moderate
🚌 C1, C2, C3, C4
♿ Few
❓ Go early if possible. Restrictions on numbers allowed in during busy periods can result in queues

Far left: *magnificent Mudéjar carvings are an attractive feature of the Reales Alcázares in Sevilla*
Left: *the restaurants and bars around the cathedral are always lively on a warm Sevillian evening*

Moorish-looking Tarifa is the continent's southern-most town

✚ 42B1

✉ 21km west of Algeciras

🍴 Choice of restaurants (£–£££)

🚌 Bus connections with Algeciras

♿ Few

↔ Roman ruins at Baelo Claudia at Bolonia (14km northwest on N340, 9km off main road to Bolonia Cove)

❓ Dia de los Reyes (6 Jan); Carnival (pre-Lent); Romeria del Consejo (15 May); Fiesta de San Juan (24 Jun); Fiesta de la Virgen del Carmen (16 Jul); National Folk Music Festival (early Aug); Fiesta de Nuestra Señora de la Luz (early Sep)

ℹ Paseo de la Alameda
☎ 956 68 09 93; www.tarifaweb.com

TARIFA ★

To stand on the Punta de Tarifa is to be at the southernmost point of Europe, with the coast of the African continent only 14km away. Located on the fringe of the Costa del Sol, Tarifa has a totally different flavour about it which in itself makes a visit worthwhile.

The town has played an important role in the history of the Iberian peninsula. It was named after Tarif Ibn Malik, the Moorish leader who in 710 arrived here from north Africa with a small band of men and took possession of the area. This led to the larger invasion which took place the following year and the subsequent Moorish conquest of most of present-day Spain. Tarifa was taken by the Christians in 1292 but the siege was maintained for the next couple of years.

Entrance to the town, which is encircled by walls, is through a Moorish gate. With its dazzling white houses and maze of narrow, winding streets, Tarifa retains a distinctive Moorish look. The port offers a good view of the old Moorish castle above the town, which is in the hands of the Spanish Navy and not open to the public.

Tarifa is blessed by a long expanse of sandy beach backed by pine trees. This marks the meeting point of the Mediterranean and the Atlantic and the strong winds which sweep across the sand create excellent conditions for windsurfing in the bay. The place has now become a top centre for the sport, with kitesurfing fast gaining in popularity.

TORRE DEL MAR ✪

Located in the eastern part of the Costa de Sol, Torre del Mar is the beach resort of Vélez-Málaga, capital of the Axarquía region.

There are unsubstantiated claims that Torre del Mar once formed part of an ancient Greek settlement known as Mainake which is believed to have been destroyed by the Carthaginians, prior to the arrival of the Romans. These days the town consists primarily of a long beach lined with a string of high-rise apartment blocks catering mainly for summer visitors.

One of the resort's most pleasant features is the extended esplanade which follows the coast, to reach the Marina of Caleta de Vélez. With over 200 berths, it presents an attractive scene of boats and yachts, offering sailing and a variety of other watersports. Its lively cafés and restaurants also provide a good place in which to idle the time away. Another bonus is the good seafood served here in numerous eateries.

✚ 47D2
✉ 30km cost of Málaga
🍴 Choice of restaurants and bars (£–£££)
🚌 Bus connections
♿ Few
🔄 Vélez-Málaga (5km inland, ➤ 90)
❓ Fiestas at Vélez-Málaga
ℹ Tourist information: Avenida de Andalucía 52
☎ 952 54 11 04

Above: *some boats at Torre del Mar bear colourful decorations*
Left: *the regular mending of his nets is essential to the livelihood of every local fisherman*

✚ 46C2

✉ 12km west of Málaga

🍴 Many pubs, restaurants, bars (£–£££)

🚌 Half-hourly to Málaga (25 minutes) and Fuengirola

♿ Few

🔁 Málaga (➤ 28), Puerto Deportivo at Benalmádena (➤ 46)

❓ Carnival (pre-Lent); Feria de Verdiales (Mar); Easter; Fiesta de la Virgen del Carmen (16 Jul); Día del Turista (early Sep); Feria de San Miguel (late Sep); Romería de San Miguel (Sun, late Sep)

ℹ Main office: Ayuntamiento, Plaza Blas Infante 1 ☎ 952 37 95 12. Plaza de la Independencia s/n ☎ 952 37 42 31. Plaza de las Comunidades Autónomas, s/n (Playa de Bajondillo) ☎ 952 37 19 09

TORREMOLINOS ⭐

Torremolinos, lying only 8km west of Málaga airport, heralds the start of the most developed part of the coast. To many, this stretch of coast, lined with high-rise apartment blocks and development as far as Estepona, represents the real Costa del Sol.

Torremolinos began to grow as a holiday resort in the 1950s, when the building of luxury hotels got under way, and it became one of the first places on this coast to cater for mass tourism. Its proximity to Málaga airport is a point in its favour. At the height of summer the resort has a great appeal for the younger set, with a reputation for its hectic night life. Out of season, however, it takes on a different mantle. The pace slows down and, at weekends in particular, the city appears almost as a suburb of Málaga with Spanish families much in evidence.

There's a definite divide between the town and the beach area below. The main artery of the town is the pedestrianised Calle San Miguel. Lined with a varied assortment of shops and surrounded by numerous bars and restaurants, this mini *ramblas* attracts a constant flow of people. Other popular spots for eating and drinking are the small Andalucian-style development of Pueblo Blanco nearby, and the area of El Calvario, located beyond the top end of San Miguel. A favourite establishment here is the Galloping Major (splendidly translated as El Comandante Galopando), which opened in 1964 as the first English-style pub in Torremolinos.

Did you know ?

A pioneer of the development of Torremolinos was an Englishman. George Langworthy (Don Jorge or El Señorito Inglés as he was called by the local people) made history when in 1930 he opened up his home, the Hacienda Santa Clara, as a residence for foreigners, creating a centre for the needy. He grew to be held in great esteem by the local people and, after his death, a street was named for him and a monument erected in his honour.

At the south end of San Miguel the Cuesta del Tajo leads down winding steps crammed with souvenir shops to the El Bajondillo beach.

The beach area shows another side of Torremolinos. With massive hotels, apartment blocks, bars and restaurants, this area is packed during the summer. To the left, the Playa de Bajondillo gives way to the beaches of Playmar and Los Almos. To the right, beyond the Castillo de Santa Clara, lie the beach areas of La Carihuela and Montemar.

The Paseo Marítimo, the seafront promenade, extends east to Playamar and west to La Carihuela, now continuing as far as Benalmádena Costa. The walk to La Carihuela offers pleasant sea views and some dramatic rock formations, before entering the old fishing village of La Carihuela, which is a delightful area of pictureque little houses and streets. It has a good reputation for excellent fish and seafood restaurants. In summer, the *chiringuitos* (beach bars) are well worth sampling.

Top: *Torremolinos is one of the coast's liveliest resorts*
Above: *La Carihuela Beach is famed for its beach bars*

A Drive to Antequera

Distance
125 km

Time
About 6 hours

Start/end point
Torremolinos
✚ 46C2

Lunch
Parador de Antequera (££)
✉ García del Olmo,
    Antequera
☎ 952 84 02 61

This drive offers some striking scenery, taking you first to Antequera and continuing to the bizarre boulders in the El Torcal National Park.

From Torremolinos turn onto the N340 towards Málaga. Passing the airport on your left, continue on the Málaga ring road (Ronda de Málaga) and follow the signs to Antequera (N331).

After the turn off to Finca de la Concepción this excellent highway climbs up through the hills of the Montes de Málaga, scattered with olive groves and tiny white houses. As you approach Antequera strange rock shapes rise from the fertile plains, noticeably the striking form of the so-called Peña de los Enamorados (Lovers' Rock). About an hour after departure you should enter Antequera (➤ 44). Allow time to explore this attractive city of churches and convents.

Take the Calle de la Legión, in a southerly direction and a few moments out of town, pause to admire the magnificent views of Antequera on your left, backed by the distinctive form of the Peña de los Enamorados. Take the C3310, following the signs to Torcal.

The expansion of Torremolinos from tiny fishing village to popular resort can be observed from the hills of Mijas

The road winds through a barren landscape of rocks and boulders for about half an hour before reaching a right turn to Parque Natural del Torcal de Antequera. As you drive through the park, the rocks and boulders become increasingly curious, until the whole landscape appears positively lunar-like. The road ends some 15 minutes later by a small hut; walking trails start from here.

Rejoin the C3310 and continue south to the coast and return to Torremolinos.

TORROX COSTA ✪

Along the eastern end of the Costa del Sol, situated between Torre del Mar and Nerja, is the resort of Torrox Costa. Torrox consists basically of a long stretch of beach, backed with modern apartment blocks, sympathetically designed with reflections of the Moorish style of architecture.

The resort has been developed primarily for summer visitors, when it bustles. The beach offers a number of watersports, while an extended promenade offers the visitor a pleasant stroll along the seafront, with a reasonable choice of restaurants, bars and shops.

You might like to take a look at the church of La Encarnación and the Hermitage of Nuestra Señora de las Nieves, both of which still retain traces of Moorish influences. Scattered along the coast are a few old watchtowers and small fortresses, going back to the times when there was a threat of pirate invasion.

Some 4km inland lies the old town of Torrox; built up the steep slopes of the hill, its whitewashed houses make an attractive pattern.

✚ 47E2
✉ 47km east of Málaga
🍴 Choice of restaurants and bars (£–£££)
🚌 Bus connections
♿ Few
↔ Competa (18km north) (► 50), Nerja (6km east) (► 69)
❓ Carnival (pre-Lent); La Cruz de Mayo (2 May); Fiesta de San Juan (23–24 Jun); Fiesta de la Virgen de las Nieves (5 Aug); local fair (4–7 Oct)
ℹ Centro Internacional, bloque 79 ☎ 952 53 02 25

Torrox, above, and the beach at Torrox Costa, right

🪧 47D2
✉ 34km east of Málaga
🍴 Many restaurants (£–£££)
🚌 Bus connections
♿ Few
↔ Nerja (► 69)
ℹ Avenida de Andalucia 119
☎ 952 54 11 04

Above: *some attractive façades can be seen in Vélez-Málaga*
Right: *a rooftop view of the town from its well-restored Moorish castle*

VÉLEZ-MÁLAGA ⭐

The small town of Vélez-Málaga lies 5km inland from Torre del Mar, surrounded by subtropical vegetation. Capital of La Axarquía, it is the centre of an agricultural region known for its production of strawberries and vineyards, which produce the muscatel grapes from which the famous Málaga wines are made. It is also a centre for the processing of olive oil and sugarcane. Ceramics feature among other industries. If you are here on a Thursday, take time to wander around its weekly market, always an enjoyable experience.

The town is crowned by a 13th-century Moorish castle which has been well restored. There are good views of the surrounding countryside from up here. The oldest part of the town, known as Arrabal de San Sebastián, is a picturesque area of narrow streets. You will also come across attractive mansions built during the 16th and 17th centuries. Of special note, among the several churches to be found in the town, is the 15th-century church of Santa María la Mayor, which shows the Mudéjar style. This was the first building to be erected by the Christians, following their victory over the Moors here in 1487.

Where To...

Above: *Nerja beach*
Right: *at Fuengirola*

91

Restaurants in Costa del Sol & Beyond

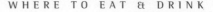

Prices

Prices are approximate, based on a meal for one, including wine and service:

€ = up to €18
€€ = €18–€35
€€€ = over €35

Eating Costs

The cost of eating out along the coast is wide open. In the more fashionable restaurants prices can be on a par with top international restaurants anywhere. However, with careful selection, you can eat very well in and around the coast at reasonable cost.

Many restaurants offer a *menú del día* (menu of the day) which includes a two- or three-course meal and normally a drink as well.The price range varies according to the category of the restaurant and the area, but you will usually get good value. In popular tourist centres quality restaurants tend to serve only à la carte. While this may cost more, the selection is greater, the quality of the food probably higher and you can still eat at affordable prices.

Platos combinados (combined plate), found in the more casual type of establishment, can fulfill the need for an adequate, low-cost meal. Some establishments also offer a *menú infantil* (child's menu), with smaller portions at reduced rates.

Almuñécar

Bodega Francisco (€)
Centrally placed bar/restaurant serving a good selection of tapas at very reasonable prices.
✉ Calle Real 15 ☎ 952 63 01 68 🕐 Lunch and dinner

Antequera

La Espuela (€€)
Long-established restaurant, within the lower part of the bullring complex. A wide selection of dishes includes local specialities.
✉ Plaza de Toros de Antequera ☎ 952 84 46 62 🕐 Lunch and dinner, closed Mon

Arroyo de la Miel

Mesón del Virrey (€€€)
In a pleasant old building. Known for good traditional cooking with emphasis on meat dishes. Summer terrace. Busy at weekends.
✉ Avenida de la Constitución 87 ☎ 952 44 35 99 🕐 Lunch and dinner, closed Wed

Ventorillo de la Perra (£££)
Housed in an 18th-century inn. Cosy, attractive patio with plants. Spanish and international dishes.
✉ Avenida de la Constitución 85 ☎ 952 44 19 66 🕐 Lunch and dinner, closed Mon

Benalmádena Costa

Malagueto Puerto (€€)
Offers good grilled meats and a wide selection of fish dishes. Bream, baked in salt, can be a good test.
✉ Puerto marina ☎ 952 44 00 04 🕐 Lunch and dinner

El Mero (€€)
Top quality restaurant located on first-floor level with views over the marina. Known for its shellfish and barbecued meats.
✉ Dársena de Levante, Puerto Marina ☎ 952 44 07 52 🕐 Lunch and dinner

El Mirador (€€€)
Top class international restaurant offering varied menu and panoramic views of the surrounding mountains and the coastline.
✉ Calle Bellavista, Urb Torremuelle (on the Fuengirola–Benalmádena coastal road) ☎ 952 44 33 98 🕐 Lunch and dinner

Benalmádena Pueblo

Casa Fidel (€€)
Rustic atmosphere with large fireplace. International cuisine.
✉ Maestra Ayala 1 ☎ 952 44 91 65 🕐 Lunch and dinner, closed Tue, Wed lunch, Aug

Córdoba

Bandelero (€–€€)
Facing the Mezquita with an attractively decorated bar and several dining rooms at the rear. Wide selection of simple dishes and tapas.
✉ Calle de Torrijos 6 ☎ 957 47 64 91 🕐 Lunch and dinner

El Churrasco (€€)
Long-standing restaurant and lively *tapas* bar. Centrally located with attractive patio. Known for grilled meats.
✉ Romero 16 ☎ 957 29 08 17 🕐 Lunch and dinner, closed Aug

Estepona

Buenaventura (€€€)
Top-quality restaurant offering creative cuisine. Outdoor dining in beautiful courtyard and out on the Plaza de la Iglesia, where diners can watch operatic

performances in August.

✉ **Plaza de la Iglesia 5**
☎ **952 85 80 69** ⏲ **Lunch and dinner**

El Cenachero (€€)

Located in the marina.
Mediterranean cuisine,
specialises in fresh shellfish,
zarzuelas, fish baked in salt.

✉ **Puerto Deportivo** ☎ **952 80
14 42** ⏲ **Lunch and dinner,
closed Tue in winter and
15–30 Nov**

Mesón Cordobés (€€)

Excellent location, with tables
out on the attractive Plaza de
la Flores. Fish features largely
on the menu: the fresh catch
of the day is a good bet when
its available.

✉ **Plaza de la Flores 15**
☎ **952 80 07 37** ⏲ **Lunch and
dinner, closed Sat**

La Rada (€)

Popular for its lively atmosphere and the quality of its
fish, seafood and rice dishes.

✉ **Avenida de España** ☎ **952
79 10 36** ⏲ **Lunch and dinner,
closed Tue**

Frigiliana
The Garden Bar (€€)

Popular with locals, offering a
casual atmosphere and
attractive views. Good for
barbecued and grilled meats.

✉ **In the old part of the town;
look for signs** ☎ **952 53 31 85**
⏲ **Lunch and dinner, closed
Tue**

Fuengirola
Crêpes 'n' Bar (€)

Small hospitable estab-
lishment offering more than
50 varieties of French-style
crêpes. Eating indoors, out
on the pavement or on the
lovely enclosed patio at
the rear.

✉ **Calle Ollerías 15** ☎ **951 31
11 77** ⏲ **Lunch and dinner,
closed Tue**

La Langosta (€€)

Long-established favourite,
renowned for lobster dishes.

✉ **Calle Francisco Cano 1, Los
Boliches** ☎ **952 47 50 49**
⏲ **Dinner only, closed Sun**

Le Vagabond (€€)

French cuisine in this friendly
restaurant. Attractive
surroundings with a small
terrace for outdoor eating in
summer. Excellent value.

✉ **Calle de la Cruz 14** ☎ **952
46 21 46** ⏲ **Dinner only, closed
Wed**

Portofino (€€)

Italian specialities and international dishes in this
restaurant on the seafront.

✉ **Edificio Perla, Paseo
Marítimo 29** ☎ **952 47 06 43**
⏲ **Lunch and dinner, closed
Mon, 1–15 Jul, 1–15 Dec. Dinner
only in summer**

Granada
Chikito (€€)

Popular restaurant, once
frequented by writers and
artists. Bar and restaurant
known for its cured ham.

✉ **Plaza del Campillo 9**
☎ **958 22 33 64** ⏲ **Lunch and
dinner, closed Wed**

Mirador de Morayma (€€€)

Excellent position with fine
views of the Alhambra from
its terraces. Country-style
decor, lively ambience.

✉ **Pianista Gracia Carillo 2**
☎ **952 22 82 90** ⏲ **Lunch and
dinner, closed Sun**

Sevilla (€€)

Old haunt of García Lorca and
Manuel de Falla. Attractive
dining rooms, open terrace.

Tapas

Tapas bars are a way of
life in Spain and a visit to
some of these
establishments in the old
part of Málaga will serve
to give a feel of the town.
A lively atmosphere is
usually provided by local
people, who meet
regularly for animated
conversation over a beer
or a chilled *fino* sherry. The
choice of *tapas* can range
from olives, almonds,
jamón serrano (cured
ham), to *tortilla* slices
(Spanish-style omelettes),
vegetable dishes, and a
selection of fish and
seafood dishes, often well
laced with garlic.

Porciones denote
smaller helpings, while
raciones are more ample
The bars are open for
most of the day to serve
drinks and food.

Budget Food

For inexpensive eating and an informal atmosphere, the coast offers a variety of options. In addition to the famous *tapas* bars, there are *bodegas*, *tabernas* and *cervecerías*, all of which are basically bars which serve food as well. Then there are the popular *chiringuitos*, casual open air beach bar/restaurants, found the length of the coast. A *marisquería* is a restaurant which specialises in seafood, while an *asado* offers barbecued food, usually meats.

✉ Oficios 12 ☎ 958 22 12 23 🕐 Lunch and dinner, closed Sun

Málaga

Adolfo (€€)

Good quality restaurant known for its excellent local and international cuisine.

✉ Paseo Marítimo Pablo Ruiz Picasso 12 ☎ 952 60 19 14 🕐 Lunch and dinner, closed Sun

Antonio Martín (€€€)

Seafront restaurant with large terrace. Long-time favourite specialising in seafood.

✉ Paseo Marítimo ☎ 952 22 73 98 🕐 Lunch and dinner, closed Sun dinner

La Cancela (€)

Two small dining rooms. Specialities include *fritura malagueña* and *ajo blanco*.

✉ Calle Denis Belgrano 3 ☎ 952 22 31 25 🕐 Lunch and dinner, closed Wed evening

Casa del Guardia (€)

One of Málaga's oldest bars, lined with barrels. A good place to sample sweet wines and great variety of *tapas*.

✉ Alameda Principal ☎ None 🕐 Lunch and dinner

Casa Pedro (€€)

Long-standing favourite with the locals. Large dining area overlooking the sea.

✉ Quitapenas 121, El Palo beach ☎ 952 29 00 13 🕐 Lunch and dinner, closed Mon dinner

El Chinitas (€€)

Lively, known for its good *tapas*. Specialises in Andalucían and Mediterranean dishes. Commemorative plaques to García Lorca outside.

✉ Calle Moreno Monroy 4-6 ☎ 952 21 0972 🕐 Lunch and dinner

La Espuela (€€)

Good local dishes in cosy, Andalucían atmosphere.

✉ Obispo Herrara Oria 5 ☎ 952 28 11 98 🕐 Lunch and dinner, closed Sun

El Figón de Bonilla (€€)

Known for its good local cooking and fish dishes.

✉ Calle Cervantes ☎ 952 22 32 23 🕐 Lunch and dinner, closed Sun

Lo Güeno (€)

Typical *tapas* bar offering a wide choice.

✉ Calle Marín García 9 ☎ 952 22 21 80 🕐 Lunch and dinner

Mesón Astorga (€€)

Known for its traditional Andalucían cooking.

✉ Calle Gerona 11 ☎ 952 34 25 63 🕐 Lunch and dinner, closed Wed

Orellana (€)

Great favourite with Malagueñians. Speciality – stuffed squid.

✉ Calle Moreno Moreno 5 ☎ 952 23 30 12 🕐 Lunch and dinner

Refectorium (€€€)

Traditional restaurant specialising in meat dishes.

✉ Calle Cervantes, 8 ☎ 952 21 89 90 🕐 Lunch and dinner

Rincón de Mata (€€)

Well known for its excellent *tapas*. Good value all round.

✉ Calle Esparteros 8 ☎ 952 22 31 35 🕐 Lunch and dinner

Marbella

El Balcón de la Virgen (€)
Delightful small restaurant housed in a 17th-century house in one of the town's picturesque little streets. Andalucian and international cuisine, with specialities that include fish stew, seafood and paprika steaks.
✉ Calle Remedios 2 ☎ 952 77 60 92 🕐 Lunch and dinner, closed Sun

California (€)
Casual ambience, popular with locals. Good value fish and seafood tapas.
✉ Calle Málaga 2, Edif. Sol. No. 2 ☎ 952 86 67 52 🕐 Lunch and dinner, closed Sun

La Hacienda (€€€)
Top restaurant with reputation for *haute cuisine*. Good location up hill with sea views.
✉ Urbanización Las Chapas, N340 (12km east of Marbella) ☎ 952 83 11 16 🕐 Dinner only in summer; closed Mon, Tue and mid-Nov to mid-Dec

Los Naranjos (€€)
Good position right on Plaza de los Naranjos, centre of Marbella's Casco Antiguo. Mediterranean and international cuisine.
✉ Plaza de los Naranjos s/n ☎ 952 77 18 19 🕐 Lunch and dinner, closed Sun

La Pesquera (€)
In the old town. Bar and restaurant serving good seafood.
✉ Plaza de la Victoria s/n ☎ 952 76 51 70 🕐 Lunch and dinner

La Pesquera del Faro (€€)
Overlooking the sea, this combines the atmosphere of a beach hotel with good-quality food. Specials include fish baked in salt and seafood dishes. Steps lead down to a terrace right on the beach, adjoining Marbella's marina.
✉ Playa del Faro, Paseo del Marítimo ☎ 952 86 85 20 🕐 Lunch and dinner

Mijas

Mirlo Blanco (€€)
Basque and international cuisine. Outdoor terrace overlooking the charming little square of Plaza de la Constitución.
✉ Paseo del Compás ☎ 952 48 57 00 🕐 Lunch and dinner

El Padtrasto (€€€)
Spectacularly sited on the clifftop. Terrace with views of Fuengirola and the coast. Top cuisine, offers local specialities and international dishes. Access by lift or a steep flight of stairs.
✉ Paseo del Compás 22 ☎ 952 48 50 00 🕐 Lunch and dinner

La Reja (€€)
Elevated position offering pleasant views of the town from the terrace. Specialises in grilled meats, fish, seafood and pizzas.
✉ Los Caños 9 ☎ 952 48 69 42 🕐 Lunch and dinner, closed Mon

Valparaíso (€€)
In an attractive villa with a terrace, gardens and a pool, this is ideal for a dinner-dancing evening out.
✉ Carretera de Fuengirola, Km 4 ☎ 952 48 59 96 🕐 Dinner only, closed Sun in winter

Nerja

La Marina (€)
Popular with locals and

What to Drink
Wine is widely drunk with meals, with a preference for red wine, sometimes taken chilled. White and rosé wines are also available and a pleasant alternative is a jug of *sangría*. Based on a combination of red wine, fruit and a liqueur, topped up with lemonade and ice, this is best enjoyed when eating out in the open air on a warm sunny day. Spain has excellent beer, fruit juices and soft drinks. An acquired taste is *Horchata*, a nonalcoholic drink based on almonds and barley.

For afters, there is a wide range of *coñacs* (Spanish brandy) ranging from the inexpensive Fundador or Terry, to the special savour of a Carlos I.

Healthy Ingredients
Olives have been cultivated since the time of the Greeks and Andalucía produces one of the most important olive crops in the world. The production of olive oil involves arduous work, from the collection of the crops towards December, to the first pressing, which is known as virgin oil. Olive oil forms an integral part of Spanish cooking and scientific research suggests it is good for the health, as is garlic, which also features widely in Spanish cuisine.

Eat Spanish

Restaurants along the coast tend to specialise in fish and seafood. Top class grilled meats and international cuisine are also much in evidence, however, with all tastes catered for. Local Andalucian cooking is more likely to be found in smaller restaurants or away from the coast and tourist areas. Here you will find an emphasis on tasty homemade soups, vegetables prepared in a variety of ways, meat and game dishes, often served as a stew.

In line with much of the country, the Andalucians tend to eat late: lunch is normally taken from about 2PM and can well carry on to early evening! Many diners will arrive around 10PM or so. The trendier the place, the later the action. Many restaurants are closed one day a week. This varies from one restaurant to another, so check if in doubt. Some may open for dinner only. Note also that some restaurants may close for a while in summer and/or during holiday periods in winter.

families, this restaurant offers a wide variety of fish dishes and seafood tapas.
✉ Plaza de la Marina ☎ 952 52 12 29 🕓 Lunch and dinner

Pepe Rico (€€€)

Top restaurant renowned for the quality of its cuisine. Housed in a mansion, meals are served in an elegant dining room or outside on a flower-filled patio.
✉ Almirante Ferrándiz 28 ☎ 952 52 02 47 🕓 Lunch and dinner, closed Tue, 1–15 Dec, 15 Jan–15 Feb

Nueva Andalucía

Divina Gula (€€)

International cuisine. Specialities include Argentinian-style grilled meats, fresh pasta dishes, lamb and fish.
✉ Plaza la Orquídea s/n ☎ 952 81 87 00 🕓 Lunch and dinner

Puerto Banús

Azul Marino (€€)

Brasserie-restaurant, good for fish and seafood.
✉ Front Line, Port I ☎ 952 81 10 44 🕓 Lunch and dinner

La Caracola del Puerto (€€)

Restaurant overlooking the quay; known for its varieties of paellas, along with a good selection of tapas and other dishes.
✉ Muelle Benabola 5 ☎ 952 81 16 84 🕓 Lunch and dinner, closed Tue

Christian Bistro du Port (€€)

One of Puerto Banús's earliest restaurants, ever popular.
✉ In the port ☎ 952 81 10 06 🕓 Lunch and dinner

Don Leone (£££)

Longtime favourite, open air, overlooking marina. Mainly Italian cuisine.
✉ Muelle Ribera ☎ 952 81 17 16 🕓 Lunch and dinner; closed end-Nov–end-Dec

La Ola (€€)

Elegant quayside restaurant specialising in paella and rice dishes.
✉ Muelle Ribera ☎ 952 81 14 23 🕓 Lunch and dinner, closed Tue

Salobreña

Mesón de la Villa (€–€€)

One of the resort's most popular restaurants, with a good reputation for its fish dishes.
✉ Plaza F. Ramírez de Madrid ☎ 958 61 24 14 🕓 Lunch and dinner, closed Wed

San Pedro de Alcántara

Albert & Simon (€€€)

Top class restaurant, known for the excellence of its creative French cuisine.
✉ Urb Nueva Alcántara (near Naturae) ☎ 952 78 37 14 🕓 Lunch and dinner, closed Sun

Jardín del Vino (€€)

On San Pedro's main street, the restaurant offers rustic surroundings, cosy ambience and international cuisine. Terrace open in summer.
✉ Marqués del Duero 9 ☎ 952 78 42 16 🕓 Lunch and dinner, closed Wed

Victor (€€)

Specialities include rack of lamb, sea bass and good seafood.
✉ Centro Comercial Guadalmina, local 1 ☎ 952 88 34 91 🕓 Lunch and dinner, closed Sun dinner and Mon

San Roque

Los Remos (€€€)
High class restaurant in a neoclassical villa with attractive gardens. Known for fish and seafood dishes.
✉ Villa Victoria S, Campamento ☎ 956 69 84 12 🕐 Lunch and dinner, closed Sun

Sevilla

La Albahaca (€€)
Housed in a typical Andalucían house, decorated with tiles and plants. Spanish and French cuisine.
✉ Plaza Santa Cruz ☎ 954 22 07 14 🕐 Lunch and dinner, closed Sun

Casa Robles (€€)
Traditional restaurant situated near the cathedral. Classic Andalucian dishes and lively tapas bar downstairs, this is a favourite with locals.
✉ Calle Álvarez Quinters 58 ☎ 954 90 32 72 🕐 Lunch and dinner

El Giraldillo (€€)
Established restaurant with excellent location facing the cathedral and Giralda. Tables out on the pavement for a casual drink and a light meal.
✉ Plaza Virgen de los Reyes 2 ☎ 954 21 45 25 🕐 Lunch and dinner

El Rincón de Pepe (€€)
Popular restaurant in the Barrio Santa Cruz. Outdoor eating in season.
✉ Calle Gloria 6, Barrio Santo Cruz ☎ 954 56 29 75 🕐 Lunch and dinner

Torremolinos

La Bodega (€)
Located right on the lively Calle San Miguel this place is constantly busy; frequented by locals and tourists.
✉ Calle San Miguel 40 ☎ 952 38 73 37 🕐 Lunch and dinner

El Chacha (€)
This open-air seafood tapas bar is a Torremolinos institution. Stand to sample its wide range of fresh fish and seafood, offered at very reasonable prices.
✉ Palma de Mallorca 3 ☎ None 🕐 Lunch and dinner

El Comedor (€€)
Stylish establishment in the picturesque Pueblo Blanco quarter. The menu is based on good quality Basque cooking.
✉ Calle Casablanca, Pueblo Blanco ☎ 952 38 38 81 🕐 Lunch and dinner, closed Sat. Weekends only in winter

Dona Francisquita (££)
Pleasant restaurant, centrally located, with a high standard of cooking and service.
✉ Calle Casablanca, Edif Zurbarán 11 ☎ 952 37 49 10 🕐 Lunch and dinner

La Jábega (€€)
This lively restaurant along the promenade serves a good choice of meat, fish and seafood.
✉ Paseo Marítimo, La Carihuela ☎ 952 38 63 75 🕐 Lunch and dinner

Med (€€)
Central restaurant. Cool sophisticated ambience. Emphasis on Mediterranean cuisine. Panoramic views.
✉ La Mercedes 12, 2a Planta ☎ 952 05 88 30 🕐 Lunch and dinner, closed Mon

Local Delicacies
A popular starter is the Andalucian speciality, *gaspacho Andaluz*, a chilled tomato soup with additions, although this is not always on the menu in winter. Other favourites are asparagus, *jamón serrano* (cured ham), *entremés de carne* (cold meats), tuna salad, *calamares a la romana* (fried squid rings).

For the main course there is often a good selection of fish dishes, although they can be pricey. *Fritura Malagueña* (an assortment of fried fish) and fish baked in salt, are specialities, while you can always ask for the catch of the day. Otherwise pork, chicken and rabbit, grilled (*a la plancha*) or prepared with a sauce, are usually a good bet. There is always *paella*, which can be taken as a first or main course.

Desserts tend to be limited, with *flan* (crème caramel), ice cream or fresh fruit of the season among the most popular choices.

Hotels in Costa del Sol & Beyond

Prices
Prices are approximate, for a double room, including breakfast and IVA (VAT):

€ = under €60
€€ = €60–150
€€€ = over €150

Hotel Gradings
Officially registered hotels in Spain range from 1 to 5 star (with an additional top deluxe category of GL, Gran Lujo). Other types of accommodation include apartment hotels, hotel residencias (no restaurant), hostels and pensions. Stars are assigned according to services and facilities available. Suites can usually be found in the 4 or 5-star range. Tariffs should be displayed.

Almuñecar
Casablanca (€)
Moorish-style hotel in a pleasant location. Spacious rooms with views over the sea or the castle and mountains behind.
 Plaza San Cristóbal
☎ 958 63 55 59

Antequera
Parador de Antequera (€)
Modern building in attractive setting amongst ruins of the Moorish fortress.
✉ García de Olmo s/n
☎ 952 84 02 61;
www.parador.es

Benalmádena Costa
Las Arenas (€)
Six-floor hotel opposite the Arroyo de la Miel and Bil Bil Castle beaches. Most rooms with sea views and terrace.
✉ Avenida Antonio Machado 22 ☎ 952 56 18 05

Triton (€€)
Long established hotel set in sub-tropical gardens, with mountain and sea views. Pools and tennis courts.
✉ Avenida Antonio Machado 29 ☎ 952 44 32 40

Córdoba
Melía Córdoba (€€€)
Pleasant and centrally located.
✉ Jardines de la Victoria
☎ 957 29 80 66;
www.solmelia.com

Mezquita (€€)
Housed in an old 16th-century house. Attractive decor, conveniently situated opposite the Mosque.
✉ Plaza Santa Cataline 1
☎ 957 47 55 85

Estepona
Atalaya Park (€€€)
Comfortable, set in attractive gardens facing the beach with sports facilities.
✉ Carretera N340 ☎ 952 88 90 00; www.atalaya-park.es

Las Dunas Beach Hotel & Spa (€€€)
On the beach, between Marbella and Estepona. Tropical gardens, Andalucían-style décor with a Middle Eastern influence. Pool, gourmet restaurant, water-sports, riding, beauty and therapy clinic.
✉ La Boladilla Baja, Ctra de Cádiz, Km 163.5 ☎ 952 79 43 45; www.las-dunas.com

Dobar (€)
Good location on the seafront. Reasonable rates.
✉ Avenida España 178
☎ 952 80 06 00

El Paraíso (€€)
Set on a hill with good views of the coast and attractive gardens, surrounded by a golf course. Large outdoor and heated pool, riding.
✉ Ctra de Cádiz, Km 134
☎ 952 88 30 00; www.hotelparaisocostadelsol.com

Santa Marta (€)
Attractive little hotel with bungalows, situated on the seafront. Shady gardens and pool with bar.
✉ Ctra de Cádiz, Km 167
☎ 952 88 81 77;
www.hotelsantamarta.com

Fuengirola
Angela (€)
Attractively decorated in a modern Andalucían style on the Paseo Marítimo, within walking distance of the beach. Shops, rail and bus transport are all near by.
✉ Paseo Rey de España s/n
☎ 952 47 52 00

Florida (€€)
One of Fuengirola's earliest hotels, this has a pool in semitropical gardens, with live music and shows during the summer.
✉ **Paseo Maritimo, s/n**
☎ **952 47 61 00**

Hostal Italia (€)
Situated in the centre of town, warm family atmosphere. Good value
✉ **Calle de la Cruz 1**
☎ **952 47 41 93**

Las Pirámides (€€)
Near the beach and town centre. Facilities include a garden and pool, flamenco shows and live music. Golf, mini golf and tennis near by.
✉ **Miquel Márquez, 43**
☎ **952 47 06 00**

Villa de Laredo (€€)
Pleasant new hotel right on the promenade.
✉ **Paseo Marítimo 42** ☎ **952 47 76 89**

Granada
Alhambra Palace (€€)
Old traditional favourite with Moorish-style décor. Close to the Alhambra with views of the Sierra Nevada from some rooms.
✉ **Calle Peña Partida, 2**
☎ **(958) 22 14 68; www.h-alhambrapalace.com**

NH Inglaterra (€)
Pleasant hotel, centrally located, housed in a 19th-century house.
✉ **Cetti Meriem 4** ☎ **958 22 15 59**

Málaga
Don Curro (€€)
Medium-range hotel, conveniently positioned between the old town and the

seafront. Within easy walking distance of Málaga's major attractions.
✉ **Sancha Lara 7** ☎ **952 22 72 00**

Los Naranjos (€€)
In residential district, near the centre. Small garden with orange trees.
✉ **Paseo Sancha, 35** ☎ **952 22 43 17**

Parador Málaga-Gibralfaro (€€)
High up the hill by Gibralfaro Castle with magnificent views of Málaga and bay.
✉ **Gibralfaro** ☎ **952 22 19 02; www.parador.es**

Marbella
Andalucía Plaza (€€)
Spacious establishment, attractively refurbished, set in gardens, two pools, casino.
✉ **Nueva Andalucia (opposite Puerto Banús)** ☎ **952 81 20 00**

Chapas Palacio del Sol (€€€)
Set in lovely pine groves, popular with families, sports and nature lovers. Tennis, mini golf, table tennis offered, with riding, golf and watersports in the locale.
✉ **Ctra de Cádiz, Km 198**
☎ **952 83 13 75**

El Fuerte (€€)
Attractive hotel in pleasant gardens. Near the sea and within walking distance of Marbella centre.
✉ **Avenida El Fuerte** ☎ **952 86 15 00; www.fuertehoteles.com**

Hotel Fuerte Miramar-Spa (€€€)
Part of the El Fuerte group, this modern hotel on the seafront has an outdoor

Travellers with Disabilities
Facilities for travellers with disabilities are little evident; however, there are signs of progress in this area. Certain hotels in the region offer fixed and mobile ramps, lifts, and wider doorways, corridors and toilets to accommodate wheelchairs and parking areas close to the hotel entrance. If such services are required, check that the hotel in question carries the wheelchair symbol and state your needs before booking.
   For further information on facilities for disabled visitors wishing to visit the area contact:
Las Gerencias Provinciales del Instituto Andaluz de Servicios Sociales (Provincial Management of the Andalucían Institute of Social Services)
✉ Avenida Manuel Agustín 26, 4, Málaga
☎ (952) 21 04 12/13/14

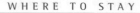

Paradores

Very pleasant accommodation is provided by the *parador*, originally denoting a lodging place for the gentry. The late 1920s saw the development of this network of state-run establishments. Often in attractively converted old castles and historic buildings, *paradores* are scattered throughout the country, making good stopovers when touring by car. There are also some purpose-built modern *paradores* in tourist centres, many set in tranquil gardens, often with a pool, in lovely surroundings. Although tariffs have risen over the years, the splendour of the buildings and their locations make an overnight stay well worthwhile.

heated pool, hydrotherapy centre and good facilities.
✉ **Plaza José Luque Manzano s/n** ☎ **952 76 84 10; www.fuertehoteles.com**

Lima (€€)

Close to the old town and a short walk to the seafront.
✉ **Avenida Antonio Belón** ☎ **952 77 05 00**

Marbella Club (€€)

Old time favourite, set in lush gardens with swimming pool.
✉ **Blvd Príncipe Alfonso de Hohenlohe** ☎ **952 82 22 11; www.marbellaclub.com**

Puente Romano (€€€)

Super deluxe village-like complex with landscaped gardens, pool, tennis.
✉ **Carretera N340, between Marbella and Puerto Banús** ☎ **952 82 09 00; www.puenteromano.com**

Riu Rincón Andaluz (€€)

Attractive hotel complex built in an Andalucían-style pueblo. Near Puerto Banús and close to the sea.
✉ **N340 Km 173** ☎ **952 81 15 17**

San Cristobal (€)

Modest, conveniently situated for Marbella centre.
✉ **Ramon y Cajal 3** ☎ **952 77 12 50**

Mijas

Hotel Mijas (€)

At the entrance to Mijas, the hotel is set amidst gardens with a pool, offering superb views down to the coast.
✉ **Urb Tamisa s/n** ☎ **952 48 58 00; www.hotasa.es**

Monda

Castillo de Monda (€€)

Old castle converted into a hotel by British proprietors. Moorish-style furnishings, stunning views of Monda and the Sierra de las Nieves.
✉ **Monda (18km northeast of Marbella)** ☎ **952 45 71 42; www.costadelsol.spa.es**

Nerja

Balcón de Europa (€€)

Old favourite located on the promenade of the same name. Private beach.
✉ **Paseo Balcón de Europa** ☎ **952 52 08 00**

Parador de Nerja (€€)

Modern *parador* set high up with pleasant gardens. Splendid views of the beach below and surrounding bay.
✉ **Almuñécar 8** ☎ **952 52 00 50; www.parador.es**

Villa Flamenca (€)

In the Nueva Nerja development some 300m from the beach with a garden and pool, restaurant and bar.
✉ **Urb. Nueva Nerja** ☎ **952 52 21 96**

Ronda

Maestranza (€€)

Situated in the centre of town, facing Ronda's old bullring, this hotel has comfortable rooms and tasteful decor. Facilities include the use of a private country club (tennis, swimming pool, squash).
✉ **Calle Virgen de la Paz** ☎ **952 18 70 72**

Reina Victoria (€€)

An old favourite, built in the early 20th century. Set in attractive gardens with swimming pool. Fine views of surrounding mountains.
✉ **Calle Jerez 25** ☎ **952 87 12 40; www.ronda.net/usuar/victoria**

San Gabriel-Su Casa en Ronda (€€)

Delightful hotel with tasteful decor, housed in an 18th-century mansion with an attractive courtyard.

✉ **Marqués de Moctezuma 19**
☎ **952 19 03 92;**
www.hotelsangabriel.com

San Pedro de Alcántara
Pueblo Andaluz (€€)

Built in typical Andalucían style, this establishment has a pool and gardens.

✉ **Avenida Luis Carillo Benítez**
☎ **952 78 05 97**

Sevilla
Alfonso XIII (€€€)

One of Spain's most famous hotels. Built around a large courtyard with arches and plenty of greenery. Unique Moorish-style with magnificent marble floors, panelled ceilings and lovely ceramic tiles. Gardens and pool.

✉ **Calle San Fernando 2**
☎ **954 22 28 50**

Bécquer (€)

Pleasant establishment. Good location, near the town centre and the river.

✉ **Calle Reyes Católicos 4**
☎ **954 22 89 00;**
www.hotelbecquer.com

Hostería del Laurel (€€)

In the heart of the picturesque Barrio de Santa Cruz. Has an outdoor restaurant in a square lined with pretty houses.

✉ **Plaza de los Venerables 5**
☎ **954 22 02 95**

Hotel Amadeus (€€)

Small hotel of great charm, with attractive decor and character. Will appeal to music lovers. Family run,

warm, welcoming ambience.

✉ **Calle Farnesio 6** ☎ **954 50 14 43**

Torremolinos
Cervantes (€€)

Large hotel a few minutes' walk from town centre. Garden with pool, rooftop pool, restaurant, casino. Live music and dancing. Undergoing extensive refurbishment at time of writing.

✉ **Calle Las Mercedes s/n**
☎ **952 38 40 33; www. hotelcervantestorremolinos.es**

Fénix (€€)

In the centre of town, with direct access to the beach. Garden and pool, sauna, gymnasium and evening entertainment.

✉ **Las Mercedes 24** ☎ **952 37 52 68**

Hostal Los Riscos (€)

Small and friendly with rooms and apartments, in a quiet residential area, near the town centre. English speaking personnel.

✉ **Calle Loma de los Riscos 40** ☎ **952 37 21 99**

Pez Espada (€€€)

This large hotel offers all comforts, with a swimming pool surrounded by gardens.

✉ **Vía Imperial 11, La Carihuela**
☎ **952 38 03 00;**
www.medplaya.com

Tropicana Hotel and Beach Club (€€€)

Colourful tropical design and layout. Kidney-shaped pool set in gardens and beach club add to its appeal.

✉ **Calle Trópico 6, La Carihuela** ☎ **952 38 66 00;**
www.hotel-tropicana .net.reservas

Rural Retreats

As a total contrast to the beach, visitors may like to venture into Andalucía's hinterland. At a short distance from the coast are to be found a number of so-called rural lodgings, which can vary from country cottages, rooms in attractive *haciendas* to mountain refuges or hostels and facilities for camping. In addition to wonderful scenery and fresh mountain air, there are often possibilities for hiking, riding and other pursuits.
Information and reservation centre:

RAAR (Red Andaluza de Alojamientos Rurales)
✉ Apdo. 2035, 04080 Almería ☎ 902 44 22 33; fax 950 27 16 78; www.raar.es
You can also contact:
AHRA (Asocación de Hoteles Rurales de Andalucía)
✉ Centro Cultural Hospital de Santiago, Calle Cristo Rey 2, 23400 Ubeda (Jaén) ☎ 953 75 58 67
Rural Andalus
✉ Calle Don Cristián 10, 29007 Málaga ☎ 952 27 62 29; fax 952 27 65 567; www.ruralandalus.es

Shopping in Costa del Sol & Beyond

Shopping in Málaga

The most concentrated shopping area in Málaga is in and around calle Marqués de Larios, north of the Alameda Principal, Málaga's main boulevard. Within easy walking distance are a host of shops and boutiques which stock a variety of goods, geared more to local needs than to visiting tourists.

If you take time to browse around, however, you will come across some very attractive ceramics and handicrafts, antiques, leather goods (shoes can be a good buy) and jewellery, in addition to the odd souvenir and gift shop.

Antique Shops

Granada
Gonzálo Reyes Muñoz
✉ Calle Mesones (Placeta de Cauchiles 1) ☎ 958 52 32 74

Málaga
A Vela Díaz
✉ San Augustín 10 ☎ 952 21 25 28

E Ruiz Linares
✉ Santa Maria 21 ☎ 952 22 80 47

El Martinete
✉ Carretería 90 ☎ 952 21 33 35

El Trianon
✉ Madre de Dios 22 ☎ 952 21 08 46

Ronda
El Portón
✉ Manuel Montero 14 ☎ 952 87 24 10

Muñoz Soto
✉ B S Juan de Dios de Córdoba 34 ☎ 952 87 14 51

San Pedro de Alcántara
Cabon s l Antiguedades
Large showroom offering an extensive range of attractive Spanish and Portugese rustic antique furniture.
✉ Ctra de Cádiz, Lm 169.5, Guadalmina Baja ☎ 952 88 28 97

Bookstores

Nerja
Nerja Book Centre
Large secondhand book store, stocking thousands of books in several different languages.
✉ Calle Granda 30 ☎ 952 52 09 08

Ceramics

Estepona
Cerámica La Chiminea
Beautiful designs created by Paco Leonicio, who learnt his crafts at Triana, one of Spain's top centres for pottery. Wide selection of decorative tiles, glazed and unglazed ceramics.
✉ Ctra Cádiz–Málaga, Km 162.2 ☎ 952 79 44 75

Málaga
Cerámica Fina
Cerámica Fina stocks attractively displayed ceramics of all kinds showing a high standard of workmanship.
✉ Calle Coronel 5, near the church of San Juan ☎ No phone available

San Pedro de Alcántara
Artesanía Troyano
Specialists in porcelain, features Lladró porcelain and other fine makes.
✉ Calle Lagasca 63. Also in Marqués del Duero ☎ 952 78 11 99

Sevilla
Sevillarte
A wide range of beautiful ceramic products at three different branches.
✉ Branches at: Gloria 5
☎ 954 21 88 35; Sierpes 66
☎ 954 21 28 36; Vida 13
☎ 954 56 29 45

Fashion

Fuengirola
Brandtex
Ladies' boutique with stylish fashionware available in all sizes. Good selection of mix and match outfits.
✉ Avenida Suel 4, Edificio Tres Coronas ☎ 952 58 25 85

Málaga
Boutique Azulay
Good selection of high quality fashionwear.
✉ **Larios 10** ☎ **952 21 75 39**

Mango
One branch of Spain's well known chain of elegant fashion stores.
✉ **Larios 1** ☎ **952 22 31 02**

Marbella
Don Miguel
Long established, with wide range of fashionwear for men and women. Some of the brand names to be found here.
✉ **Avenida Ricardo Soriano 5** ☎ **952 77 31 40**

Gucci
No introduction needed. Elegant range of men's and women's clothing.
✉ **Calle Valdéz 8** ☎ **952 86 14 99**

Louis Feraud
Fashion clothes by Feraud, known for their striking designs and vibrant colours.
✉ **Plaza Victoria** ☎ **952 82 81 06**

Nerja
Bruna Cavvalini
Some good bargains may be had in this fashionable ladies' boutique. Sportswear and more formal gear available, plus accessories. Clothes from Sevilla and London.
✉ **Calle Barrio** ☎ **952 52 30 58**

Mostaza
Mainly for men. Casual and formal wear. Good for shirts and sweaters, suits and jackets.
✉ **Calle Diputación Provincial 6** ☎ **952 52 14 00**

Puerto Banús
Boutique Donna Piu
Italian-style fashion.
✉ **Paseo Benabola L87** ☎ **952 81 49 90**

Boutique Number One
Specialises in French and Italian designer collections.
✉ **Levante 1** ☎ **952 81 16 97**

Gianni Versace
Just the job for the fashion conscious, men's and women's fashions.
✉ **Centro Comercial Benabola 8** ☎ **952 81 02 96**

Torre del Mar
Singh
Elegant boutique for women's and men's clothes. Top fashion names, with the latest designs.
✉ **Calle Avenida de Andalucía 121** ☎ **952 54 10 91**

Food and Wine Shops

Puerto Banús
Club de Gourmet
Exciting range of unusual products, aimed at gourmet visitors. Next to Bar Inglés.
✉ **By entrance to Puerto Banús, near El Corte Inglés** ☎ **952 81 78 00**

San Pedro Alcántara
Andrés Ingelmo Marcos
Quality Iberian ham and sausages, also cheeses from Zamora and Valladolid and Rioja wines.
✉ **c/ Miguel Hernández 4** ☎ **952 78 65 56**

Puerto Banús
Puerto Banús is a very different shopping scene These former orange-growing farmlands were developed in the sixties by the businessman Don José Banús to become the successful international centre it is today.
For those who like to shop at trendy boutiques stocked with designer goods, against the glamorous background of yachts and a chic ambience, Puerto Banús is a veritable mecca – at a price!

Department Stores

The mammoth department store has become a sign of the times in Spain and an increasing number are to be found on the Costa del Sol. El Corte Inglés is a household name in Spain. It started trading way back in 1939, selling only English fabric. Over the years the group has expanded into a large chain of stores located all over Spain and selling an increasing range of items 'made in Spain'.

Gift Shops

Benalmádena (Puerto Marina)

La Maison

Ideal stopping off place for a variety of small gifts such as porcelain items and ceramic fish.

✉ **Puerto Marina** ☎ 952 56 0299

Fuengirola ✂

Regalos de Arte Maxi

Attractive choice of Lladró porcelain, ceramics from Sevilla, Majorcan pearls and a good selection of easy to carry gifts.

✉ **Avenida Ramón y Cajal 1** ☎ 952 47 33 34

Málaga

Original

A variety of gifts made in wood, including reproductions of music boxes and antique toys.

✉ **Calle Calderia 2, and Calle Marín García 6** ☎ **None**

Marbella

Dupar

Local distributors of Lladró and Majorica. Wide range of gifts.

✉ **Avenida Ramón y Cajal 3** ☎ **None**

Torremolinos

Las Tres Torres

Offers a good choice of products, including a wide range of items made in Toledo steel, ceramics and pottery from Sevilla, and an attractive selection of Majorcan pearls.

✉ **Calle San Miguel 17** ☎ 952 21 79 39

Montinas Gift Shop

A wide variety of attractive gifts available. Official agents for Lladró, Majorica and Swarovski.

✉ **La Nogalera 26** ☎ 952 38 11 78

Regalos Geni

Wide range of gifts, including good selection of Lladró, Swarovski crystal and Joseph Bofill sculpture.

✉ **Calle San Miguel 8** ☎ 952 38 28 05

Jewellery

Fuengirola

Nicholson

Specialises in modern jewellery designs; selection of earrings, bracelets, pendants and other items. Another shop in Marbella's Orange Square.

✉ **Calle Marbella s/n** ☎ 952 47 58 82

Marbella

Joyería Don Lal

Extensive selection of jewellery and watches, all attractively displayed. Also has branches in Puerto Banús, Ribera 167, Casa OPQ and Torremolinos, San Miguel 48.

✉ **Avenida Ramón y Cajal 3** ☎ 952 86 66 53

San Pedro de Alcántara

Anthony's Jewellers

Unusual and original designs by the owner, with many pieces incorporating semi-precious stones.

✉ **Plaza las Faroles** ☎ 952 78 62 74

Torremolinos

Joyería San Miguel

Good selection of all types of jewellery and watches.

✉ **San Miguel 11** ☎ 952 38 05 53

Leatherware

Benalmádena
Artesanía Piel
Leather goods produced on the premises. Out of the ordinary belts and handicrafts.
✉ **Puerto Marina** ☎ **None**

Fuengirola

Bravo
Good reputation for shoes, handbags, luggage and leather accessories. Shops also in Marbella and Torremolinos.
✉ **Avenida Condes de San Isidro 33** ☎ **952 46 17 19**

Málaga
Nuñez Antilope
Nuñez Antilope is an old leather factory stocking suede and leather gear.
✉ **Bolsa s/n** ☎ **952 21 27 45**

Rosselli
Good selection of leather shoes and bags, for women and men.
✉ **Calle Molino Larios** ☎ **952 21 43 23**

Marbella
Charles Jourdan
Wide range of shoes and leather goods. Other items include jewellery, umbrellas and sun glasses.
✉ **Avenida Ramón y Cajal** ☎ **952 77 00 03**

Nerja
Colectivo Artesanal Manos
Specialists in leatherware goods.
✉ **Pintada 8** ☎ **None**

Torremolinos
Zerimar
Specialises in handbags, traditional leather goods and raw silk outfits.
✉ **Bulto 49** ☎ **None**

Stores

Málaga
El Corte Inglés
Six floors of fashion, gifts, exhibitions of arts and crafts.
✉ **Avenida de Andalucia 4–6**
☎ **952 30 00 00**

Felix Saenz
Wide range of goods available from inexpensive to sophisticated.
✉ **Felix Saenz Plaza s/n**
☎ **952 22 56 00**

Málaga Plaza Centro Comercial
American-style complex with a variety of quality shops.
✉ **Armengual de la Mota 12**
☎ **952 61 40 40**

Rosaleda
A light, spacious centre with over 100 shops including a bookstore, hairdressers, a supermarket, various interior furnishing shops, 14 cinema screens and a video club.
✉ **Centro Rosaleda, Avenida Simon Bolivar** ☎ **952 88 05 00**

Marbella
La Cañada Commercial Centre
Centre with individual shops, fast food restaurants and a supermarket.
✉ **Parque Comerical la Cañada, Ctra de Ojén s/n**
☎ **952 86 01 42**

Puerto Banús
Costa Marbella Department Store
Gigantic superstore, just outside town. Part of the El Corto chain, with a hypermarket (Hipercor) on the ground floor and specialised shops on the upper floors.
✉ **Ctra N340, Km 174** ☎ **952 90 99 90**

Markets
Street markets in Spain are great fun to visit. Major centres along the coast have a weekly market, generally open from early in the morning to around 2:30PM.

Attractive displays of fruit and vegetables create a profusion of colour. In addition to enjoying the lively ambience of clamour and bustling activity, there is always the chance of picking up a bargain. Popular items for bringing back as gifts include pottery and ceramics, leatherware, straw baskets, hats and the occasional piece of costume jewellery.

Children's Activities

Fun for Kids

Spaniards are known for their fondness for children, who can expect to be treated with courtesy and made to feel welcome.

There is plenty to amuse youngsters down on the Costa. Apart from the obvious pleasures of the beach or pool, which may suffice for some, the area has many attractions aimed at entertaining young visitors of all ages. Amusement and aqua parks offer all kinds of entertainment such as water slides, kamikaze rapids and wave pools. Some aqua parks are closed in the winter, so check this out.

The Sea Life Centre at Benalmádena's Marina, demonstrations of birds of prey, the zoo at Fuengirola, and the fun rides in mini trains around some of the main centres are also worth considering.

Children are also sure to enjoy the fun and colour of a local fiesta, should the opportunity arise.

Benalmádena
Selwo Marina

This new type of marina/fauna park contains Andalucía's first dolphinarium and penguinarium. Exhibitions feature dolphins, sea lions and exotic birds. 3D cinemas and a children's playground offer plenty of fun all round.

✉ Parque de la Paloma s/n Benalmádena ☎ 902 19 04 82 ◷ Daily 10–6 🖐 Moderate 🍴

Tivoli World, Arroyo de la Miel

This show and amusement park, set in extensive grounds, is a great favourite with families, especially at the weekend. In addition to numerous rides and amusements (including a giant rollercoaster), visitors can enjoy flamenco shows, a Wild West Town, theatre and live music. Two recent additions are Tivolilandia, an infant area, and Tivoli Agua, which contains a water mountain flume ride.

✉ Avenida de Tivoli s/n, Arroyo de la Miel ☎ 952 57 70 16 ◷ April, May, 15–30 Sep, Oct daily 4PM–1AM; Jun, 1–14 Sep 5pm–2am; Jul–Aug 6PM–3AM; Nov–Mar 11AM–9PM (times subject to change) 🖐 Moderate 🍴 Restaurants (£–££) 🚃 RENFE station Arroyo de la Miel 🚌 Arroyo de la Miel 🚶 Few

Benalmádena Costa
Sea Life Benalmádena

This sea life centre takes you on an exciting voyage of discovery to the bottom of the ocean. From the shallow waters to the depths of the sea you can enjoy close views of a whole wealth of marine life, ranging from tiny shrimps and starfish to giant stingrays and great sharks. There are also presentations and feeding displays. An area dedicated to the sea horse is a delightful new addition.

✉ Puerto Deportivo, Benalmádena ☎ 952 56 01 50 ◷ Daily 10–6 🖐 Moderate 🍴 Restaurant (££) 🚃 RENFE station Benalmádena 🚶 Good

Banalmádena Pueblo
Jardín de las Aguílas (Eagle Gardens)

Up the hill, in the Castillo de Aguílas, is the Birds of Prey Centre, where demonstrations are held with eagles, owls, falcons and vultures. Next door is a miniature castle, Castillo Colombo, and a reptile sanctuary, Snake City.

✉ Castillo de Aguílas just before Benalmádena Pueblo ☎ 952 56 82 39 ◷ Show times daily: Oct–Apr, 1, 5; May, Jun, 1, 6, 7, 8; Jul, Aug, 1, 6, 8 subject to weather 🖐 Moderate 🚌 Bus to Benalmádena Pueblo 🚶 Good

Estepona
Selwo Aventura

A safari park where you can see a whole range of animals from the five continents of the world, roaming around in a semi-wild habitat. Much of the circuit is made by truck.

✉ Autovía Costa del Sol, Km 162.5, Las Lomas del Monte ☎ 902 19 04 82 ◷ Jan–May, Oct–Dec daily 10–6; Jun–Sep 10–7 🖐 Moderate 🚌 Direct to Selwo (Costa line) 🚶 Few

Fuengirola
Zoo Fuengirola

Spectacular modern new zoo, designed to re-create the natural habitat of all the species living here. Wander among tropical forests, rivers and waterfalls to glimpse its varied flora and fauna, including chimpanzees, crocodiles, numerous birds and reptiles. Restaurants and a children's area all contribute to a wonderful family outing.

✉ Camolio José Cela, 6 Fuengirola ☎ 952 66 63 01 🕐 Daily 10–6 💵 Moderate 🚉 RENFE station Fuengirola

Marbella
Funny Beach Marbella
Family leisure centre offering mostly water activities, including go-kart races, water bikes, 'ski' banana, quad trips.

✉ Ctra. Cádiz, 340 Marbella ☎ 952 82 33 59 🕐 Daily 11–11 💵 Free 🚌

Mijas Costa
Parque Acuático Mijas (Aqualand)
This water theme park has great watershoots, including a thrilling Kamikaze, pools, slides and rapids.

✉ Ctra N340, Km 290 ☎ 952 46 04 09 🕐 May, daily 10–5:30; Jun, Sep 10–6; Jul, Aug 10–7; closed Oct–Apr 💵 Expensive 🍴 Restaurant (££) 🚌 Fuengirola bus station 🛗 Few

Puerto Banús
Super Bonanza
The *Bonanza* departs every two hours from midday onwards for a cruise along the coast.

✉ Sinatra Bar, Puerto Banús ☎ 952 38 56 00

Torre del Mar
Parque Acuático Aquavelis
Another fun water park that the children will enjoy.

✉ Urb El Tomillar ☎ 952 54 25 92 🕐 Daily 10–6 💵 Moderate 🚌 Bus from Málaga (Torre del Mar stop) 🛗 Few

Torremolinos
Aquapark
Aquatic attractions here include giant water chutes, water mountains and artificial waves bearing names such as Kamikaze, Cresta Run and Waikiki Surf. The Aquapark also boasts a mini park, restaurant and boutique.

✉ Ctra de Circunvalación (near Palacio de Congresos) ☎ 952 38 88 88 🕐 Jul–Sep daily 10–6, Dec–Feb 10–5 💵 Moderate 🍴 Restaurant 🚉 RENFE station Torremolinos 🚌 🛗 Few

Crocodile Park
Centrally located in Torremolinos, the park features more than 300 crocodiles of all ages and sizes, which can be viewed at close quarters. Guided visits with a crocodile trainer available. Children under 12 must be accompanied by an adult.

✉ Calle Cuba, 14 Torremolinos ☎ 952 05 17 82 🕐 Shows: Wed 5:30, Jun–Oct 6 💵 Expensive 🚉 Nearby 🚌 Nearby 🛗 Few

Club El Ranchito
An impressive Andalucian horse spectacular. The show includes dressage, the use of horses for herding bulls and dancing horse demonstrations.

✉ Senda del Pilar 4, Colima ☎ 952 38 31 40 🕐 Shows: Wed 5:45, Jun–Oct 6 💵 Expensive 🚉 Nearby 🚌 Nearby 🛗 Few

Take Care
When taking children down to southern Spain do remember to take sensible precautions against too much exposure to the sun. It can be exceedingly hot during the summer months, so that protective hats and effective sun lotions are highly advisable.

Costa del Sol & Beyond Attractions

Nightlife

The Costa is famed for its lively night scene, with an abundance of discotheques and nightclubs to suit every taste. There is a concentration of discos in Torremolinos, with a wide choice of glitz to be found in and around the Marbella area, especially Puerto Banús. In Fuengirola and Los Boliches you can find many bars with music, and perhaps a sing-song, a number of which are English-run.

Opening times are flexible; however, the action starts late, very late, with minimal activity to be expected before 11PM or midnight. Once things hot up they seem to carry on well into the early hours. Charges are variable, with some discos charging a fairly substantial entrance fee, which usually includes one free drink.

Casinos

Benalmádena Costa
Casino Torrequebrada
American and French roulette, Black Jack, Punto Blanco, slot machines and private gaming room. Dress is formal and passports must be shown.

✉ Avenida del Sol s/n ☎ 952 44 60 00 🕐 Daily 8PM–4AM 🚌 Bus stop Benalmádena Costa 💷 Expensive

Nueva Andalucía
Casino Marbella
American and French roulette, Black Jack, Stud Caribbean poker, Punto Blanco, slot machines. Jacket and tie for men. Passport required.

✉ Hotel Andalucía Plaza, opposite Puerto Banus, Nueva Andalucía ☎ 952 81 40 00 🕐 Daily 9PM–3AM 🚌 Bus stop Andalucía Plaza 💷 Expensive

Casino Nueva San Roque
Chic casino offering roulette and Black Jack, Passport, jacket and tie required.

✉ Ctra N340, Km127 ☎ 965 78 10 00

Cinema and Theatre

Among the various cinemas and theatres along the coast, which can be enjoyed by locals and visitors alike, one place stands out as a rock of entertainment for the English-speaking community in the area. The Salon Variétés, which first opened in Fuengirola in 1985, continues to put on a variety of entertainment each season, which is from the middle of September to mid-June. Audiences can enjoy all types of plays, from thrillers to comedies, musicals and pantomines, concerts, flamenco shows and dance festivals, and lectures.

Fuengirola
Cine Sohail
✉ Avenida Condes de San Isidro s/n ☎ 952 47 46 41

Salon Variétés
Cinema and theatre with regular plays and entertainment for the English-speaking community.
✉ Emancipacón 30 ☎ 952 47 45 42

Málaga
Alameda Multicines
✉ Córdoba 13 ☎ 952 21 34 12

Albéñiz Multicines
✉ Alcazabilla 4 ☎ 952 21 58 98

América Multicines
✉ Explanada de la Estación ☎ 952 33 99 91

Andalucía Cinema
✉ Victoria 2 ☎ 952 21 06 16

Astoria Cinema
✉ Plaza de Maria Guerrero ☎ 952 21 20 64

Echegaray Cinema
✉ Echegaray 13 ☎ 952 21 39 99

Sala Cánovas
Theatre, opera and concerts are performed here in winter with the Málaga Symphony Orchestra.
✉ Plaza del Ejido s/n ☎ 952 25 72 00

Teatro Miguel de Cervantes
Major cultural centre with year round programme.
✉ Ramos Martín s/n ☎ 952 22 41 00

Puerto Banús
Cine Gran Marbella
You can often see films in English at this multiplex.
✉ Puerto Banús ☎ 952 81 00 77

Sevilla
Teatro Municipal Alameda
Varied programme of plays.
✉ Calle Crédito 13 ☎ 954 90 01 62

Teatro Lope de Vega
For classical concerts.
✉ Avenida María Luisa s/n ☎ 954 59 08 53

Dance Clubs

Fuengirola
Discoteca Superstar
✉ Calle Jacinto Benavente s/n C 952 47 04 92

Málaga
Varsovia
Popular with all age groups.
✉ Calle José Denis Belgrado 5 ☎ No phone

Piano Club Georges
✉ Mar 90 ☎ 952 22 82 39

Surf
✉ Calle S Nicolás 2 ☎ 952 22 74 83

Marbella
Disco Willy Salsa
Popular with the younger set.
✉ Ctra Cadiz, Km 178 ☎ 952 82 73 63

Oh! Marbella
A real hot spots, with good views from the terrace.

Hotel Don Carlos, Ctra de
Cádiz, Km 192 ☎ 952 83 54 77

Olivia Valere
A Costa del Sol favourite. Passport required.
✉ Ctra de Istán, Km 0.8 ☎ 952 82 88 45

Torremolinos
New Mario
Favoured by an older set.
✉ Calle Casablanca ☎ 952 37 50 37 🕔 Closed Mon

Palladium
A popular spot, with trendy lighting and loud music.
✉ Avenida Palma de Mallorca 36 ☎ 952 38 42 89

Piper Discoteca
Funky music, young crowd.
✉ Avenida de Mallorca ☎ No phone 🕔 Closed Mon

Flamenco and Jazz

Benalmádena Costa
Fortuna Nightclub
International show, flamenco and dancing to live bands.
✉ Casino Torrequebrada, N340 between Benalmadena Costa and Carvaja ☎ 952 44 60 00 🕔 From 9:30PM

Córdoba
Mesón Flamenco La Bulería
An old favourite for flamenco.
✉ Pedro López 3 ☎ 957 48 38 39 🕔 Starts at 10:30PM, closed in summer

Fuengirola
Moochers Jazz Club
Very popular café and restaurant. Live music every evening in summer, from jazz to rock. Terrace.
✉ Calle de la Cruz 17 ☎ 952 47 71 54 🕔 Dinner only

Flamenco
Flamenco is closely associated with Andalucía, where its roots belong. For the visitor who wishes to get the flavour of something seen as 'typically Spanish' there are plenty of nightspots along the Costa with flamenco shows which can be colourful and entertaining. The real magic of flamenco, however, is spontaneity and the right ambience, which is not so easy to find. You could experience some good flamenco at a local fiesta, or tucked away in the back streets of towns such as Sevilla or Málaga accompanied, ideally, by someone who knows where to look.

Jazz

Jazz fans have plenty of opportunities to indulge their interest as numerous cafés and piano bars in the main resorts, in particular Torremolinos, Fuengirola, Marbella and Puerto Banús, offer live music which can include jazz, blues and soul. Concerts are also laid on for visiting musicians. These take place in a variety of venues, such as clubs or some of the more prominent hotels along the coast.

The Mississippi-style paddleboat *Willow*, moored in the bay of Puerto Marina Benalmádena, holds jazz concerts by international artists, in addition to regular performances of their own 'resident' Willow Dixieland Band (▶ 109). Enthusiasts can check with local newspapers for a programme of events.

Granada

Jardines Neptuno

Popular but high quality flamenco shows.

✉ Calle Arabia ☎ 958 425 11 12 🕐 Daily from 10PM

Málaga

Gloria Bendita

Nightclub with live flamenco shows.

✉ Avenida Cánovas del Castillo, La Malagueta ☎ 952 22 72 79

Teatro Cervantes

The flamenco shows attract an enthusiastic audience.

✉ Ramos Marín ☎ 952 22 41 00

Vista Andalucía

✉ Avenida de los Guindos s/n ☎ 952 23 11 57 🕐 Tue–Sun 10:30PM–6AM, closed Mon

Manilva

Septima Cielo (Seventh Heaven

Bar/restaurant/creperie, with New Orleans jazz night every Wednesday.

✉ Río de Manilva 7 (between Manilva and Estepona) ☎ 952 89 26 90

Marbella

Ana Maria

In the heart of Marbella's old town, this place has a lively bar, with evening flamenco shows, along with other entertainment.

✉ Plaza Santo Cristo 5, Casco Antiguo ☎ 952 77 56 46

La Caseta del Casino

Shows of flamenco dancing and *sevillanas*.

✉ Casino Nueva Andalucía, Andalucía Plaza Hotel, N340, Nueva Andalucía. ☎ 952 81 40 00 🕐 From midnight in summer

Nerja

El Colonio

Restaurant with performances of flamenco in attractive Andalucían house.

✉ Granada 6 ☎ 952 52 18 26 🕐 Dinner show: summer, Wed–Fri 9:30 or 10PM; winter, Wed 9PM

Ronda

Casa Santa Pola

Shows in attractive restaurant, including flamenco, Spanish clasical and regional dances.

✉ Calle Santo Domingo 3 ☎ 952 87 93 28 🕐 Shows: Sat, Sun 9:30PM

Sevilla

El Arenal

Lavish theatre and restaurant with daily flamenco shows.

✉ c/Rodo 7 ☎ 954 21 64 92 🕐 Shows: 9PM and 11:30PM

Los Gallos

Small and intimate, considered to be among the top shows.

✉ Plaza de Santa Cruz ☎ 954 21 69 81 🕐 Shows 9 and 11PM

Torremolinos

El Vito de Trini

Regular flamenco shows.

✉ Centro Comercial Duquesa de España 342, Km 222,9 ☎ 952 37 23 70

Molino de la Bóveda

Flamenco and South American guitar music.

✉ Cuesta del Tajo 8 ☎ 952 38 11 85

Taberna Flamenco Pepe López

Well known venue for flamenco.

✉ Plaza de la Gamba Alegre ☎ 952 38 12 84 🕐 Apr to autumn, daily at 10PM

Sport

Along the Costa del Sol bullfights are held on Sunday afternoons during the summer season in Málaga, Estepona and Marbella. The bigger names, however, are attracted by Sevilla, Córdoba and other prominent towns in Andalucía.

Other spectator sports include soccer, basketball, tennis and golf, including the World Cup, the Spanish and the Ryder cups. Polo matches are held in Sotogrande from July to September. Check with local publications for details of matches and events.

Adventure Activities

Explore the hinterland by jeep on a day's mini-safari, which will take you over mountainous terrain, and through parklands.

Born to be Wild Adventures (Eco Tours)
Nature tours by jeep, designed for the whole family to enjoy together.
✉ **Marbella** ☎ **639 72 02 56**

Marbella Rangers Jeep Safaris
☎ **952 83 30 82**

Biking

Explore the countryside by bicycle, mountain bike, moped or motorbike.

Motomercado
✉ **Calle Sant Rosa 18, Los Boliches, Fuengirola** ☎ **952 47 25 51. Branches in Torremolinos, Benalmádena and Marbella. Routes recommended if required.**

In the Air

Aviación del Sol
Hot-air balloon trips offering spectacular views of the Serranía de Ronda Departure just after dawn, four passengers only, with champagne picnic served on return. Trips subject to weather conditions.
✉ **Ronda–Servilla (A376), Km 114.5** ☎ **952 87 72 49**

These two clubs near Málaga offer hang-gliding and paragliding courses for beginners; tandem flights with an instructor.

Club Escuela Parapente el Valle
✉ **Valle de Abdalajís** ☎ **952 48 91 80**

Club Vuelo Libre Málaga
✉ **Valle de Abdalajís** ☎ **952 48 92 98**

Flysurfing

Introduced a few years ago, flysurfing, or kitesurfing, has become a lifestyle for some on the Costa del Sol. Good spots, with favourable conditions are in Torrox, Chilches, Málaga (El Palo and El Candado), Guadalmar, Los Alamos and Playamar, between Málaga and Torremolinos, Benalmádena, Mijas Costa (El Chaparral, La Cale, Cabo Pino), Marbella (El Rosario, Guadalmina) and Estepona or Manilva's beaches.

Andalucian Aeriel Sports Federation
☎ **952 60 13 61.**

Golf

Green fees vary according to season (▶ 113 for a rough

Benalmadena Cable Car
One of the coast's great attractions is the 'Telecabina, or Teleférico Benalmádena'. From its starting point, by Tivoli World (Arroyo de la Miel), this 4-person cable car carries you up to the summit of the Calamorro mountain (about 10 minutes). Lookout points offer panoramic views of the whole coast and the Málaga mountains and marked paths offer walks in the area.

Telecabina Benalmádena SA
✉ **Explanada Tivoli s/n, Arroyo de la Miel** ☎ **952 57 50 38/902 19 04 82**

Costa del Golf

This stretch of coast is often described as the Costa del Golf, as indicated by the occasional signpost along the road. In fact golf has had a tremendous impact on the Costa del Sol area, especially during the winter season. Its mild winter climate, combined with an abundance of high quality courses, make it a highly desirable year-round golfing destination, sometimes described as the Costa del Golf.

Spain's hosting of the Ryder Cup in 1997 brought great prestige to the area, earning it international acclaim. It was a matter of great pride to the Costa that the Valderrama Golf Course in Sotogrande was the first course selected outside the UK and US to host this great international event.

Since then, the region has continued to host numerous international golfing events, attracting top players from all over the world.

guide). The majority of golf clubs require a handicap certificate. Courses get booked up by members so visitors are advised to book well in advance. Numerous competitions are open to visitors throughout the year. Useful publications include:
Golf in Andalucía
✉ Calle Calvario 8, Marbella ☎ 952 82 89 76
Revista Costa Golf
✉ Apartado Correos 358, Torremolinos. *The Federación Andaluza de Golf*
✉ Calle Sierra de Grazalema 33, bloque 5, 29016 Málaga ☎ 952 22 55 99/90

The following include some of the major clubs in the region. A number of new courses along the coast are planned. Most of the clubs offer classes and instruction by professionals.

Alhaurin Golf & Country Club (£)
Two 18 hole courses and a 9 hole, par 72.
✉ Ctra Mijas–Alhaurín, Alhaurín el Grand, Km 6 ☎ 952 59 59 70

Aloha Golf Club (£££)
18 and 9 holes, par 72.
✉ Urb Aloha, Nueva Andalucia ☎ 952 90 70 85

Los Arqueros (££)
18 holes, par 72. This course was Severiano Ballesteros' first design and offers a challenge to golfers of all handicaps.
✉ Finca Torre, Ctra de San Pedro–Ronda, C339, Km 5, Benahavis ☎ 952 78 46 00

Atalaya Golf and Country Club (£££)
18 holes, par 71 and 72

✉ Ctra Benahavis, Km 0.7, Estepona ☎ 952 88 28 12

Cabopino Golf (££)
Modern design with fine views of the coast. 18 holes, par 70.
✉ Urb. Artola Atta s/n, Km 194 Marbella ☎ 952 85 02 82

La Cala (££)
Two 18 hole courses, par 72 and 73.
✉ La Cala de Mijas, Mijas–Costa ☎ 952 66 90 33

La Dame de Noche (£)
9 holes, par 70. A 24-hour course. Floodlighting enables golfers to play at night as well as by day.
✉ Camino del Angel, Río Verde, Marbella ☎ 952 81 81 50

La Duquesa (£)
18 holes, par 72.
✉ Urb El Hacho, Ctra de Cádiz. N340, Km 150, Manilva ☎ 952 89 04 25

El Paraíso (££)
18 holes, par 72.
✉ Ctra de Cádiz. N340, Km 167, Estepona ☎ 952 88 38 46

Estepona Golf (£)
18 holes, par 72.
✉ Ctra de Cádiz. N340, Km 150 ☎ 952 11 30 81

Guadalhorce Club de Golf (£)
18 and 9 holes, par 72.
✉ Ctra de Cártama, Km 7, Campanillas ☎ 952 17 93 68

Guadalmina Club de Golf (££)
Two 18 hole courses and a 9 hole, par 72.
✉ Urb Guadalmina Alta, San Pedro de Alcántara ☎ 952 88 33 75

Marbella Golf Club (££)
18 holes, par 72.
⊠ Urb. El Roasrio, Ctra de Cádiz, N340, Km 192, Marbella
☏ 952 83 05 00

Mijas Golf International (££)
18 and 18 holes, par 71 and 72.
⊠ Urb Mijas Golf, Mijas Costa
☏ 952 47 68 43

Miraflores Golf (£)
18 holes, par 70. Right up in the hills of Mijas.
⊠ Urb. Riviera del Sol, Ctra de Cádiz, N340, Km 199, Mijas Costa
☏ 952 93 19 60

Montemayor Golf Club (££)
18 holes, par 70.
⊠ Avenida Montemayor, Benahavis ☏ 952 93 71 11

Los Naranjos (££)
18 holes, par 72.
⊠ Apdo 64, Nueva Andalucía
☏ 952 81 24 28

Parador del Golf (£)
18 holes, par 72.
⊠ About 1 km from Málaga airport ☏ 952 38 12 55

La Quinta Golf & Country Club (££)
27 holes, par 72. Fine views of the mountains and Marbella coastline. Training programmes for beginners and more advanced players, also special courses for groups.
⊠ Ctra San Pedro–Ronda. C339, Km 3 ☏ 952 76 23 90

Real Club de Club Sotogrande (£££)
18 and 9 holes, par 72. Beautiful course designed by Robert Trent.
⊠ Paseo del Parque, Sotogrande ☏ 956 78 50 14

San Roque (£££)
18 holes, par 72.
⊠ Urb San Roque Club, Ctra de Cadiz, N340, Km 127, San Roque
☏ 956 61 30 30

Santa Maria Golf & Country Club (£)
18 holes, par 72.
⊠ Coto de los Dolores, Urb Elvira. Between Fuengirola and Marbella ☏ 952 83 10 36

Torrequebrada (££)
18 and 9 holes, par 72.
⊠ Ctra de Cádiz, N340, Km 220, Benalmádena Costa ☏ 952 44 27 41

Valderrama (£££)
18 holes, par 72.
⊠ Ctra de Cádiz, N340, Km 132, Sotogrande ☏ 956 79 12 00

Horseriding

Estepona
Finca Siesta
Offers picnic and beach rides as well as a range of lessons in dressage and showjumping.
⊠ Km 163 on N230 (opposite Hacienda Beach) ☏ 952 79 01 89

Marbella
Club Hípico Elviria
⊠ El Platero, between Marbella and Fuengirola
☏ 952 83 52 72

Marbella Club Hotel
A new equestrian centre, offering lessons and rides.
⊠ Boulevard Principe Alfonso de Hohenlohe ☏ 952 82 98 84

Los Monteros Hotel
Provides lessons and rides taking in the surrounding hills.
⊠ Ctra de Cádiz, N340, Km 177
☏ 952 11 25 53

Golf
Green fees for golf courses on the Costa del Sol are considered to be amongst the most competitive in Europe. Many hotels also offer their guests reduced green fees. The following gives an approximate range of current green fees (subject to change):

£   = up to €60
££ = €60–E90
£££ = over €90

Polo
Another string to Sotogrande's bow is the sport of polo, which continues to thrive. Top ranking players come here to take part in the numerous matches which are held regularly during the summer months at the Santa María Polo Club. The sport has a substantial following, attracting an enthusiastic crowd. Although a traditional sport, with continuity within families, efforts are being made to popularise the sport and to bring it within reach of a wider public.

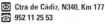

Clean Beaches

In the mid 1980s a decree was passed in Andalucía establishing the standards to be maintained with regard to the cleanliness of its beaches. The matter is taken very seriously and carefully monitored by the authorities, with the result that an ever increasing number of beaches can be seen proudly displaying the coveted Blue Flag. Beaches are classified by 5 to 1 stars according to their condition. Symbols also indicate the 'dos and don'ts', while other signs advertise services available on the beach. Visitors are requested to observe these golden rules: be sure to use a protective sun block, especially where children are concerned; drink plenty of liquid (but do check if the water is safe to drink); make sure any food consumed has been bought in a reputable place; keep the beaches clean by using containers for rubbish disposal; use a mat or towel when relaxing on the sand; do not swim in prohibited areas; respect the 'dangerous to swim' sign; do not take pets onto the beach; camp only in authorised areas which have proper facilities.

San Pedro de Alcántara
Lakeview Equestrian Centre
Qualified instruction in dressage and showjumping; private or group lessons.
✉ **Valle del Sol** ☎ **952 78 69 34**

San Roque
The San Roque Club Equestrian Centre
For beginners and experienced riders. One hour or full day hacks.
✉ **San Roque Club Suites Hotel, Ctra Cádiz, Km 126.5** ☎ **956 61 32 32**

Sotogrande Polo
You can experience the thrill of riding top class polo ponies on Sotogrande's polo fields.
☎ **956 79 64 64**

Torre del Mar
Lavao Villalba
✉ **J Ctra V Alméria s/n** ☎ **952 54 14 43**

Torremolinos
Hípica International
Lessons in dressage and jumping. One hour hacks for experienced riders (2,000 ptas). Refreshments available.
✉ **Camino de la Sierra** ☎ **952 43 55 49**

González-Garrido
✉ **J Ctra de Cádiz s/n** ☎ **952 38 30 63**

Club El Ranchito
Full horse riding facilities available (► 107).
✉ **Camino del Pilar, La Colima** ☎ **952 38 31 40**

For futher information about horse riding in rural Andalucía contact:

Asociación de Empresarios de Turismo Equestre de Andalucía (AETEA)
✉ **Isla de la Cartuja s/n, 41092 Servilla** ☎ **954 46 00 01**

Tennis
Most top hotels along the coast have tennis courts, especially in and around Marbella. Hotel guests have priority in renting the courts. There are also a number of tennis clubs in the area. The following includes a selection of these.

Benalmádena Costa
Club de Tenis Torrequebrada
✉ **Urb Torrequebrada, Ctra de Cádiz** ☎ **952 44 60 00**

Estepona
Club de Tennis Estepona
10 courts, 3 floodlit; hard and tennis-quick.
✉ **Urb Forest Hill** ☎ **952 80 15 79**

Fuengirola
Aztec Tennis Club Riviera del Sol
Tennis lessons available.
✉ **Urb. Riviera del Sol, Libra s/n** ☎ **952 93 44 77**

Marbella
Club El Casco
8 clay courts, including 2 coin-operated floodlit courts.
✉ **Urb El Rosario** ☎ **952 83 76 51**

Centro de Tenis Don Carlos
11 courts, 4 floodlit; clay and tennis-quick.
✉ **Urb Elvíria, Ctra de Cádiz** ☎ **952 83 17 39**

Club Hotel Los Monteros
10 courts, 2 floodlit.
✉ **Ctra de Cádiz, Km 194** ☎ **952 77 17 00**

Manolo Santana Raquets Club
✉ Ctra de Istán, Km 2, Marbella ☎ 952 77 85 80

Club Puente Romano
5 clay courts, 4 quick-surface and 2 artificial grass courts. Several courts are also floodlit.
✉ Hotel Puente Romao, Ctra de Cádiz ☎ 952 82 61 03

Mijas
Lew Hoad Campo de Tenis
8 courts, tennis-quick. Clinics and courses are also available.
✉ Ctra de Mijas ☎ 952 47 48 58

San Pedro de Alcántara
El Madroñal Tennis Club
✉ 7km along the San Pedro to Ronda road ☎ 952 78 53 07

Watersports

Sailing
The major marinas dotted along the coast have excellent sailing facilities. Most of the marinas and their yacht clubs organise beginners' sailing, monitor and yacht-master classes in summer. Major marinas and yacht clubs include:

La Duqesa	☎ 952 89 01 00
Estepona	☎ 952 80 18 00
Marbella	☎ 952 77 57 00
Fuengirola	☎ 952 46 80 00
Benalmádena	☎ 952 44 30 48
Málaga	☎ 952 22 63 00

Scuba Diving
Almuñecar and Nerja, east of Málaga, are good centres for diving. Day courses with fully qualified instructors are available at:
Centro Buceo Tarifa
A wide range of diving courses, day and night.
✉ Calle Alcalde Juan Nuñez 10 ☎ 956 68 16 48

Club Nautico Diving Centre
Year-round courses, equipment hire included. Daily trips from the marina.
✉ Puerto Marina de Benalmádena ☎ 952 56 07 69

Fuengirola Diving Centre
Complete PADI courses available
✉ Fuengirola port ☎ 952 58 83 12

Swimming
The beaches of the Costa del Sol vary from sand to fine grit and chinglo. Some of the best sandy beaches are around Torremolinos, Fuengirola and on either side of Marbella, all of which can become very crowded in the summer season. For more secluded beaches try the coast east of Málaga or west of Estepona.

Waterskiing and Windsurfing
There are plenty of opportunities for waterskiing and windsurfing along the western coast of Costa del Sol. Facilities and tuition are available in all major resorts, often from the hotels. The top spot for windsurfing is at Tarifa, where strong winds provide favourable conditions.

Aky Okapy
✉ Calle Ave María 7, Tarifa ☎ 956 68 53 56

Club Mistral
Wind boards for rent on the beach. Lessons available.
✉ Hotel Hurricane, Tarifa Ctra N340, Km 77 ☎ 952 68 49 19

Sierra Nevada
The Sierra Nevada is the most southerly ski resort in Europe and one of the highest, which gives it a long season (sometimes lasting well into May). Its proximity to the coast gives the possibility of swimming in the sea and skiing on snowy slopes on the same day!

The resort is easily accessible by car from Málaga (161km) and from Granada (35km) which also operates a daily bus service to the centre.

Sol y Nieve (Sun and Snow)
This ski resort offers good facilities, with ski-lifts and chair-lifts, a tourist complex and all kinds of skiing.

✉ 35km from Granada and some 100km from the coast
🕐 Dec–Apr

What's On When

Festivals

Year round, Spaniards delight in their *ferias* and *fiestas*. With their colour and exuberance they are celebrations of life itself. Many are religious events, such as Holy Week and Corpus Christi. There are pilgrimages, celebrations for patron saints, lively fairs and festivals connected with fishermen and the sea. Flamenco fairs and bullfight festivals, concerts and numerous cultural events add to the list.

Verdiales

Worth seeing, if possible, is a performance of the *Verdiales*, who are unique to the province of Málaga. These musicians form groups known as *pandas*, and are led by an *alcalde* (mayor) with a beribboned baton. Their outfits, music and dancing are most unusual and involve much flag waving. They participate in various celebrations in addition to the main festival of the *Verdiales* held in late December.

January

Los Reyes Magos (6 January). In Málaga. The Three Kings throw sweets to children from grand floats.

February/March

Carnaval (the week before Lent). In Málaga, Granada and Antequera. An exuberant affair with floats, colourful costumes, music and dancing.

March/April

Semana Santa (Holy Week, moveable date). In Sevilla, Málaga and Granada. From Palm Sunday to Easter Day there are nightly processions of *cofradías* (brotherhoods) carrying images of the saints or the Virgin; wearing pointed hoods, each carries a lighted candle. The muffled drums are accompanied by the occasional *saeta* (an improvised religious lament).

April

Fería de Sevilla (Seville Fair). Originally a cattle fair, the Fair has evolved into a world famous event of colour, music and dancing. The daily horseback parade is a special attraction with the men in dashing outfits, and their ladies decked out in traditional flamboyant dresses. Every afternoon bullfights take place in the Maestranza ring with the most famous of Spain's matadors.

May

Las Cruces de Mayo (early May). This represents an ancient custom when crosses decorated with both real and paper flowers are placed in the streets and squares. The fiesta is

particularly attractive in Torrox and Coín.

May/June

Corpus Christi (moveable date). Processions along flower strewn streets. Especially colourful in Granada, with parades, music and dancing.

July

La Virgen del Carmen (16 July). Most spectacualr at Los Boliches, Fuengirola; also at Estepona, Marbella and Nerja. The patron saint of fishermen is paraded through the streets before being taken around the bay on a boat; fireworks, music and dancing on the beach.

September

Pedro Romero Fiestas (early September). Ronda celebrates the bullfighter with *corridas Goyescas* (Goya-style bullfights), with top matadors in the costume of Goya's time.

October

Feria del Rosario. This fair is celebrated in Fuengirola during the first two weeks in October. *Casetas* (club-houses) of various societies and brotherhoods set up between Fuengirola and Los Boliches offer shows, food and drink. A lively affair, with horse-riding events, flamenco and fireworks.

December

Fiesta de Verdiales (29 December). In La Venta de San Cayetano, in Puerto de la Torre, Málaga. Colourfully attired *pandas* (musical groups) compete with each other; a lively event with music, food and wine.

Practical Matters

Above: *Fuengirola harbour*
Right: *a matador, Mijas*

117

GMT	Spain	Germany	USA (NY)	Netherlands
12 noon	1PM	1PM	7AM	1PM

BEFORE YOU GO

WHAT YOU NEED

		UK	Germany	USA	Netherlands
● Required	Some countries require a passport to remain valid for a minimum period (usually at least six months) beyond the date of entry – contact their consulate or embassy or your travel agent for details.				
○ Suggested					
▲ Not required					
Passport/National Identity Card		●	●	●	●
Visa (regulations can change – check before your journey)		▲	▲	▲	▲
Onward or Return Ticket		▲	▲	●	▲
Health Inoculations		▲	▲	▲	▲
Health Documentation (reciprocal agreement document) (➤ 123, Health)		●	●	●	●
Travel Insurance		○	○	○	○
Driving Licence (national – EU format/national/Spanish trnsltn/interntnal)		●	●	●	●
Car Insurance Certificate (if own car)		●	●	●	●
Car Registration Document (if own car)		●	●	●	●

WHEN TO GO

Average figures for Costa del Sol

High season

Low season

16°C	17°C	18°C	21°C	23°C	27°C	29°C	29°C	27°C	23°C	19°C	17°C
JAN	FEB	MAR	APR	MAY	JUN	JUL	AUG	SEP	OCT	NOV	DEC

Wet	Cloud	Sun	Sunshine & showers

TOURIST OFFICES

In the UK
Spanish Tourist Office,
22/23 Manchester Square,
London W1U 3PX
☎ (020) 7486 8077
Fax: (020) 7486 8034

In the USA
Tourist Office of Spain,
666 Fifth Avenue 35th,
New York, NY 10103
☎ (212) 265 8822
Fax: (212) 265 8864

Tourist Office of Spain,
8383 Wilshire Boulevard,
Suite 960,
Beverley Hills, Cal 90211
☎ (323) 658 7188
Fax: (323) 658 1061

WHEN YOU ARE THERE

ARRIVING

Most visitors to the Costa del Sol arrive at Málaga Airport (☎ 952 04 88 04). Spain's national airline, Iberia (☎ 302 40 05 00), operates direct scheduled flights to Málaga from major European and North American cities. The other nearest airport is Seville.

Málaga Airport Kilometres to city centre	Journey times
10 kilometres	🚆 12 minutes
	🚌 20 minutes
	🚗 20 minutes

Seville Airport Kilometres to city centre	Journey times
8 kilometres	🚆 N/A
	🚌 20 minutes
	🚗 20 minutes

MONEY

The euro is the single currency of the European Monetary Union, which has been adopted by 12 member states including Spain. Euro banknotes and coins were introduced in January 2002. There are banknotes for 5, 10, 20, 50, 100, 200 and 500 euros, and coins for 1, 2, 5, 10, 20 and 50 cents, and 1 and 2 euros. Euro traveller's cheques are widely accepted. Spain's former currency, the peseta, went out of circulation in February 2002.

TIME

Spain is one hour ahead of Greenwich Mean Time (GMT+1), but from late March until the Saturday before the last Sunday in October, summer time (GMT+2) operates.

CUSTOMS

YES
From another EU country for personal use (guidelines)
800 cigarettes, 200 cigars, 1 kilogram of tobacco
10 litres of spirits (over 22%)
20 litres of aperitifs
90 litres of wine, of which 60 litres can be sparkling wine
110 litres of beer

From a non-EU country for your personal use, the allowances are:
200 cigarettes OR
50 cigars OR
250 grams of tobacco
1 litre of spirits (over 22%)
2 litres of intermediary products (eg sherry) and sparkling wine
2 litres of still wine
50 grams of perfume
0.25 litres of eau de toilette

The value limit for goods is 175 euros

Travellers under 17 years of age are not entitled to the tobacco and alcohol allowances.

NO

Drugs, firearms, ammunition, offensive weapons, obscene material, unlicensed animals.

UK	Germany	USA	Netherlands
952 21 75 71	952 21 24 42	952 47 48 91	952 27 99 54
(Málaga)	(Málaga)	(Fuengirola)	(Málaga)

WHEN YOU ARE THERE

TOURIST OFFICES

Costa del Sol
● Costa del Sol Tourist Board
☎ 952 05 86 94/95; www.
visitacostadelsol.com

Towns/Resorts
● Plaza San Sebastian 7,
Antequera
☎ 952 70 25 05

● Avenida Antonio Machado
10, Benalmádena Costa
☎ 952 44 12 95

● Avenida San Lorenzo 1,
Estepona
☎ 952 80 09 13

● Avenida Jesús Santos
Rein 6, Fuengirola
☎ 952 46 74 57;
www.fuengirola.org

● Pasaje de Chinitas 4,
Málaga
☎ 952 21 34 45

● Glorieta de la Fontanilla,
Marbella
☎ 952 77 14 42;
www.marbella.es

● Calle Puerta del Mar 4,
Nerja
☎ 952 52 15 31

● Avenida Marqués del
Duero 69, San Pedro de
Alcántara
☎ 952 78 52 52

● Avenida de Andalucía 52,
Torre del Mar
☎ 952 54 11 04

● Ayuntamiento, Plaza Blas
Infante 1, Torremolinos
☎ 952 37 95 12

NATIONAL HOLIDAYS

J	F	M	A	M	J	J	A	S	O	N	D
2	1	1	1	1	1	1	1		1	1	3

1 Jan	New Year's Day
6 Jan	Epiphany
28 Feb	Andalucian Day (regional)
Mar/Apr	Maundy Thursday, Good Friday, Easter Monday
1 May	Labour Day
24 Jun	San Juan (regional)
25 Jul	Santiago (regional)
15 Aug	Assumption of the Virgin
12 Oct	National Day
1 Nov	All Saints' Day
6 Dec	Constitution Day
8 Dec	Feast of the Immaculate Conception
25 Dec	Christmas Day

OPENING HOURS

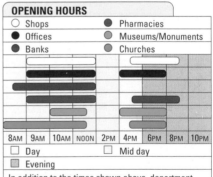

○ Shops ● Pharmacies
● Offices ○ Museums/Monuments
● Banks ○ Churches

| 8AM | 9AM | 10AM | NOON | 2PM | 4PM | 6PM | 8PM | 10PM |

☐ Day   ☐ Mid day
■ Evening

In addition to the times shown above, department
stores, large supermarkets and shops in tourist
resorts open from 10AM through to 8, 9 or even 10PM.
Most shops close Sunday and some in August. Most
banks open 9–2 (Mon–Fri). Some banks open Sat 9–2
(Oct–May). The opening times of museums can vary:
some open longer in summer, while hours may be
reduced in winter. Many museums close Sunday
afternoon, some also on Saturday afternoon, as well
as Monday or another day in the week. Some
museums offer free entry to EU citizens (take your
passport). **All opening times are subject to change.**

DRIVE ON THE RIGHT

TOILETS CHARGE ★★ ★★

PUBLIC TRANSPORT

 Internal Flights The national airline, Iberia, plus the smaller Aviaco, operate an extensive network of internal flights. The main office of Iberia is at Calle Molina Larios 13, Málaga (☎ 952 13 61 47). For reservations on domestic flights (☎ 901 33 31 11). Not cheap but worth considering if in a hurry.

 Trains Services are provided by the state-run company – RENFE. Fares are among the cheapest in Europe. A useful service is the coastal route from Málaga to Fuengirola, via Torremolinas and Benalmádena, with a stop at the airport. Trains run every 30 minutes between 6AM and 11PM (RENFE Málaga ☎ 952 12 82 63 or 952 36 02 02).

 Buses There is a comprehensive and reliable bus network operated by different companies along the coast and to inland towns and villages. Fares are very reasonable. Go to the local bus station for details of routes. The bus station in Málaga (☎ 952 35 00 61) is just behind the RENFE train station.

 Ferries A service runs from Málaga to Melilla (Morocco), run by Trasmediterránea Málaga (☎ 902 45 46 45), taking 10 hours. A shorter route to Morocco is from Algeciras to Ceuta (1¼ hours) and Tangier – via Gibraltar – (2½ hours) run by ISNASA (☎ 956 65 37 06), Trasmediterránea (☎ 956 66 52 00), and Transtour (☎ 956 65 37 06).

 Urban Transport Traffic in the main towns and resorts of the Costa del Sol is normally heavy, especially in summer, but public transport in the form of buses is generally good. From the RENFE station there is a bus which runs every 10 minutes or so to the city centre.

CAR RENTAL

 The leading international car rental companies operate on the Costa del Sol and you can hire a car in advance (essential at peak periods) either direct or through a travel agent. Airlines may offer 'fly-drive' deals. Hiring from a local firm, though, is usually cheaper.

TAXIS

 Only use taxis which display a licence issued by the local authority. Taxis show a green light when available for hire. They can be flagged down in the street. In cities and large towns taxis are metered; where they are not, determine the price of the journey in advance.

DRIVING

 Speed limits on *autopistas* (toll motorways) and *autovías* (free motorways): **120kph**; dual carriageways and roads with overtaking lanes: **100kph**. Take care on the N340 coastal highway. Cars travel at tremendous speed and this road is labelled as a dangerous one.

 Speed limits on country roads: **90kph**

 Speed limits on urban roads: **50kph**; in residential areas: **20kph**

 Must be worn in front seats at all times and in rear seats where fitted.

 Random breath-testing. Never drive under the influence of alcohol.

 Fuel (*gasolina*) is available in four grades: *Normal* (92 octane); *Super* (98 octane); *Sin plomo* (unleaded, 95 and 98 octane); and *gasoleo* or *gasoil* (diesel). Petrol prices are fixed by the Government and are similar to those in the UK. Most take credit cards.

 If you break down with your own car and are a member of an AIT-affiliated motoring club, call the Real Automóvil Club de España, or RACE (☎ 915 94 74 00, fax 915 94 72 49) for assistance. If the car is hired you should follow the instructions in the documentation; most international rental firms provide a rescue service.

CENTIMETRES

INCHES

PERSONAL SAFETY

Snatching of handbags and cameras, pick-pocketing, theft of unattended baggage and car break-ins are the principal crimes against visitors. Any crime or loss should be reported to the national police force (Policía Nacional) who wear brown uniforms. Some precautions:

- Do not leave valuables on the beach or poolside
- Place valuables in a hotel safety-deposit box
- Wear handbags and cameras across your chest
- Avoid lonely, seedy and dark areas at night

Police assistance:
☎ **091**
from any call box

TELEPHONES

All telephone numbers throughout Spain now consist of nine digits (incorporating the former area code, preceded by 9), and no matter where you call from you must always dial all nine digits. Most public telephones take coins and phonecards (*tarjetas telefónicas*) which are sold at *tabacos* or post offices for 6 or 12 euros. Some also accept credit cards.

International Dialling Codes

From Spain to:	
UK:	00 44
Germany:	00 49
USA:	00 1
Netherlands:	00 31

POST

Post Offices
Post offices (*correos*) are generally open as below; in main centres they may open extended hours. Málaga's main post office is at Avenida de Andalucía 1. Stamps (*sellos*) can also be bought at tobacconists (*estancos*). Open: Mon–Sat 9–2 (1PM Sat)
☎ 902 29 72 97 (Málaga)

ELECTRICITY

The power supply is: 220/230 volts (in some bathrooms and older buildings: 110/120 volts).

 Type of socket: round two-hole sockets taking round plugs of two round pins.
British visitors will need an adaptor and US visitors a voltage transformer.

TIPS/GRATUITIES

Yes ✓ No ✗		
Restaurants (if service not included)	✓	5–10%
Cafés/bars	✓	change
Taxis	✓	2–3%
Tour guides	✓	change
Porters	✓	change
Chambermaids	✓	change
Hairdressers	✓	change
Cloakroom attendants	✓	change
Theatre/cinema usherettes	✓	change
Toilets	✓	change

PHOTOGRAPHY
What to photograph: the rugged coast, unspoilt inland villages, examples of Moorish architecture, and panoramas of the Sierra Nevada.
Best times to photograph: the summer sun can be too bright at the height of the day making photos taken at this time appear 'flat'. It is best to take photographs in the early morning or late evening.
Where to buy film: film (*rollo*/*carrete*) and camera batteries (*pilas*) are readily available from tourist shops, department stores and photo shops.

HEALTH

Insurance
Nationals of EU countries are entitled to some free medical treatment in Spain with the relevant documentation (Form E111 for Britons) although private medical insurance is still advised and is essential for all other visitors.

Dental Services
Dental treatment normally has to be paid for in full as dentists operate privately. A list of *dentistas* can be found in the yellow pages of the telephone directory. Dental treatment should be covered by private medical insurance.

Sun Advice
The sunniest (and hottest) months are July and August when daytime temperatures are often into the 30's C. Try to avoid the midday sun and use a high-factor sun cream to start with, and allow yourself to become used to the sun gradually.

Drugs
Prescriptions and non-prescription drugs and medicines are available from pharmacies (*farmácias*), distinguished by a large green cross. They are able to dispense many drugs which would be available only on prescription in other countries.

Safe Water
Tap water is chlorinated and generally safe to drink; however, unfamiliar water may cause mild abdominal upsets. Mineral water (*agua mineral*) is cheap and widely available. It is sold *sin gas* (still) and *con gas* (carbonated).

CONCESSIONS

Students/Youths Holders of an International Student Identity Card (ISIC) may be able to obtain some concessions on travel, entrance fees etc, but the Costa del Sol is not really geared up for students (special facilities and programmes are limited). The main advantage for students and young people is that low-cost package deals are available.

Senior Citizens The Costa del Sol is an excellent destination for older travellers – travel agents offer tailored package holidays. In the winter months there are special low-cost, long-stay holidays for senior citizens; the best deals are available through tour operators who specialise in holidays for senior citizens.

CLOTHING SIZES

Spain	UK	Rest of Europe	USA		
46	36	46	36		
48	38	48	38		
50	40	50	40		
52	42	52	42		Suits
54	44	54	44		
56	46	56	46		
41	7	41	8		
42	7.5	42	8.5		
43	8.5	43	9.5		
44	9.5	44	10.5		Shoes
45	10.5	45	11.5		
46	11	46	12		
37	14.5	37	14.5		
38	15	38	15		
39/40	15.5	39/40	15.5		
41	16	41	16		Shirts
42	16.5	42	16.5		
43	17	43	17		
34	8	34	6		
36	10	36	8		
38	12	38	10		
40	14	40	12		Dresses
42	16	42	14		
44	18	44	16		
38	4.5	38	6		
38	5	38	6.5		
39	5.5	39	7		
39	6	39	7.5		Shoes
40	6.5	40	8		
41	7	41	8.5		

- Remember to contact the airport or airline on the day prior to leaving to ensure that the flight details are unchanged.
- There is no airport departure tax to pay.
- Spanish customs are usually polite and normally easy to negotiate.

LANGUAGE

Spanish is one of the easiest languages. All vowels are pure and short (as in English). Some useful tips on speaking: 'c' is lisped before 'e' and 'i', otherwise hard; 'h' is silent; 'j' is pronounced like a gutteral 'j'; 'r' is rolled; 'v' sounds more like 'b'; and 'z' is the same as a soft 'c'. English is widely spoken in the principal resorts but you will get a better reception if you at least try communicating with Spaniards in their own tongue. More extensive coverage can be found in the AA's *Essential Spanish Phrase Book* which lists over 2,000 phrases and 2,000 words.

hotel	*hotel*	breakfast	*desayuno*
room	*habitación*	toilet	*lavabo*
single/double	*individual/doble*	bath	*baño*
one/two nights	*una/dos noche(s)*	shower	*ducha*
per person/per	*por persona/por*	en suite	*en su habitación*
room	*habitación*	balcony	*balcón*
reservation	*reserva*	key	*llave*
rate	*precio*	chambermaid	*camarera*

bank	*banco*	American dollar	*dólar*
exchange office	*oficina de cambio*		*estadounidense*
post office	*correos*	bank card	*tarjeta del banco*
cashier	*cajero*	credit card	*tarjeta de crédito*
money	*dinero*	giro bank card	*tarjeta de la caja*
coin	*moneda*		*postal*
foreign currency	*moneda extranjera*	cheque	*cheque*
change money	*cambiar dinero*	traveller's cheque	*cheque de viajero*
pound sterling	*libra esterlina*	giro cheque	*cheque postal*

restaurant	*restaurante*	snack	*merienda*
bar	*bar*	starter	*primer plato*
table	*mesa*	dish	*plato*
menu	*carta*	main course	*plato principal*
tourist menu	*menú turístico*	dessert	*postre*
wine list	*carta de vinos*	drink	*bebida*
lunch	*almuerzo*	waiter	*camarero*
dinner	*cena*	bill	*cuenta*

aeroplane	*.avión*	ferry	*transbordador*
airport	*aeropuerto*	port	*puerto*
train	*tren*	ticket	*billete*
… station	*estación de ferro-*	… single/return	*ida/ida y vuelta*
	carril	… first-/second-	*primera/segunda*
bus	*autobús*	class	*clase*
… station	*estación de*	timetable	*horario*
	autobuses	seat	*asiento*
… stop	*parada de autobús*	non-smoking	*no fumadore*

yes	*sí*	help!	*ayuda!*
no	*no*	today	*hoy*
please	*por favor*	tomorrow	*mañana*
thank you	*gracias*	yesterday	*ayer*
hello	*hola*	how much?	*¿cuánto?*
goodbye	*adiós*	expensive	*caro*
good night	*buenas noches*	open	*abierto*
excuse me	*perdóneme*	closed	*cerrado*

INDEX

Acknowledgements
The Automobile Association wishes to thank the following photographers, libraries and associations for their assistance in the preparation of this book: **MARY EVANS PICTURE LIBRARY** 10, 14a, 14b, 65; **SPECTRUM COLOUR LIBRARY** 19, 52/3, 83; **www.euro.ecb.int/** 119 (euro notes); **ZEFA PICTURES LTD** 1, 17.

The remaining photographs are held in the Association's own library (**AA PHOTO LIBRARY**) with contributions from: **P BAKER** 122c; **M CHAPLOW** f/cover d (Torre); **S DAY** f/cover b (windsurfer), b/cover; **J EDMANSON** 5b, 7, 20b, 26, 27a, 32, 51, 53, 63, 84, 87/8; **A MOLYNEUX** f/cover a (ceramic plate), e (flamenco), 20a, 41, 80, 82; **K PATERSON** f/cover, oranges; **J POULSEN** 16, 21, 37a, 37b, 45, 50b, 62, 73a, 75; **D ROBERTSON** f/cover g (guitarist), 2, 8a, 8c, 11, 12, 15a, 22, 40, 44, 64; **JA TIMS** f/cover c (statue), f (pedalo), 5a, 6, 8a, 8d, 9a, 9b, 15b, 18, 24, 24/5, 27b, 28, 29, 31, 33a, 34a, 34b, 35, 36, 38, 39, 43, 48, 49, 50a, 50/5, 56, 57, 58, 59a, 61, 66/7, 67a, 68, 69, 70, 71, 72, 74, 77, 78, 79, 85a, 85b, 87, 88, 89a, 89b, 90a, 90b, 91a, 91b, 117b, 122a, 122b; **W VOYSEY** 13, 23, 60, 73b, 76, 117a.

Author's Acknowledgements
Mona King would like to thank the Costa del Sol Tourist Board, Torremolinos, Turismo de Sevilla, the Spanish Tourist Office, London, Hotel Andalucía Plaza, Marbella, Hotel Cervantes, Torremolinos Castillo de Monda, Monda, and Hotel Reina Victoria, Ronda for their assistance with this book.

Contributors
Updater (2002): Mona King **Page Layout:** Design 23 **Indexer:** Marie Lorimer
Revision Management: Outcrop Publishing Services Limited, Cumbria

Dear Essential Traveller

Your comments, opinions and recommendations are very important to us. So please help us to improve our travel guides by taking a few minutes to complete this simple questionnaire.

You do not need a stamp (unless posted outside the UK). If you do not want to cut this page from your guide, then photocopy it or write your answers on a plain sheet of paper.

Send to: **The Editor, AA World Travel Guides, FREEPOST SCE 4598, Basingstoke RG21 4GY.**

Your recommendations...

We always encourage readers' recommendations for restaurants, nightlife or shopping – if your recommendation is used in the next edition of the guide, we will send you a *FREE* AA *Essential* **Guide** of your choice. Please state below the establishment name, location and your reasons for recommending it.

_____

_____

_____

_____

Please send me **AA *Essential*** _____

About this guide...

Which title did you buy?
AA *Essential* _____
Where did you buy it? _____
When? m m / y y

Why did you choose an AA *Essential* Guide? _____

_____

_____

_____

_____

Did this guide meet your expectations?
Exceeded ☐   Met all ☐   Met most ☐   Fell below ☐
Please give your reasons _____

_____

_____

_____

continued on next page...

Were there any aspects of this guide that you particularly liked? _____

_____

_____

Is there anything we could have done better? _____

_____

_____

About you...

Name (*Mr/Mrs/Ms*) _____

    Address _____

_____

_____ Postcode _____

Daytime tel nos _____

Please only give us your mobile phone number if you wish to hear from us
about other products and services from the AA and partners by text or mms.

Which age group are you in?
    Under 25 ☐ 25–34 ☐ 35–44 ☐ 45–54 ☐ 55–64 ☐ 65+ ☐

How many trips do you make a year?
    Less than one ☐ One ☐ Two ☐ Three or more ☐

Are you an AA member? Yes ☐ No ☐

About your trip...

When did you book? m m / y y , When did you travel? m m / y y
How long did you stay? _____
Was it for business or leisure? _____
Did you buy any other travel guides for your trip?
    If yes, which ones? _____

Thank you for taking the time to complete this questionnaire. Please send it to us as soon as
possible, and remember, you do not need a stamp (*unless posted outside the UK*).

Happy Holidays!